ICE CUBE TRAY
RECIPES

ICE CUBE TRAY RECIPES

75 Easy and Creative Kitchen Hacks
for Freezing, Cooking, and Baking
with Ice Cube Trays

Jen Karetnick

Skyhorse Publishing

Skyhorse Publishing books may be purchased in bulk at special discounts for sales promotion, corporate gifts, fund-raising, or educational purposes. Special editions can also be created to specifications. For details, contact the Special Sales Department, Skyhorse Publishing, 307 West 36th Street, 11th Floor, New York, NY 10018 or info@skyhorsepublishing.com.

Skyhorse® and Skyhorse Publishing® are registered trademarks of Skyhorse Publishing, Inc.®, a Delaware corporation.

Visit our website at www.skyhorsepublishing.com.

10 9 8 7 6 5 4 3 2 1

Library of Congress Cataloging-in-Publication Data is available on file.

Cover design by Qualcom
Cover photo credit: Jen Karetnick

Print ISBN: 978-1-5107-4370-0
Ebook ISBN: 978-1-5107-4374-8

Printed in the United States of America

Contents

Introduction

How to Use This Book

Ice cube trays. You've seen them in your grandparents' freezer, right? Or if you're a member of Generation X or older, you remember them yourself: the flimsy white rectangles, one stacked upon another, that no one ever refilled so there was never any ice in them. If there were cubes in them, they always tasted freezer-burned or like the stews and soups that your grandmother made sometime before the turn of the millennium and stored in mismatched take-out containers right next to (or below or beneath) the ice cubes.

Well, home cooks still store big-batch soups and such in the freezer. But other than that, times have changed, and ice cube trays have transmuted along with them. Reformed and rehabilitated, the ice cube trays of today are forged in both hard, unbreakable plastic and flexible, food-grade silicone. They come in colors that range from pastel to neon, from black and white to primary reds and blues, and in sizes and shapes inspired by mixology, exercise, and nutrition trends from all over the world.

Indeed, now right in your own home, you can make two-inch spherical balls or two-inch squares of ice, like the slow-melting kind you'd find in a glass of bourbon at a chic hotel somewhere. You can find trays that freeze in shapes that are long and thin, ideal for fitting into a water bottle that you'd take on a jog or a bike ride. You can make and freeze your own baby food in portion-appropriate sizes. Create cubes of latte for your iced coffee that won't dilute it—or save the remaining half cup of your morning smoothie instead of throwing it away. And then there are the novelty trays that take their cues from everything from nature and holidays to popular shows, movies, books, and toys. One day you can make skull ice cubes for Halloween; the next, LEGO cubes for a child's themed birthday party.

The appearance of these trays on the market has opened the door to a larger creative realm for home cooks. Because many of them are made from FDA-certified, BPA-free, baking-grade silicone, you can not only freeze in them, but you can also cook in them. In fact, you can take these trays straight from the freezer and put them into the oven. So if you make brownies, for example, but don't want to bake all of them right away, well, here's one way you can store some of the extra batter that makes perfect sense.

As a result, anything you can make in a muffin tin or a mold, you can also make in an ice cube tray. It just takes a little ingenuity! You've probably seen a few pictures here and there on cooking and design websites. Finally, here's a book that not only provides the exact instructions on how to do it yourself—as well as what *not* to do—but it gives you additional ideas on how to tweak the 75 recipes. So really, in *Ice Cube Tray Recipes: 75 Easy and Creative Kitchen Hacks for Freezing, Cooking, and Baking with Ice Cube Trays,* you're getting about five ways to cook every recipe.

The recipes are divided into six main sections. **Infusions and Decorations** are pretty, flavored ice cubes that won't water down your drinks. **Soups and Smoothies** are work-friendly recipes that you can blend in the morning straight from the freezer or carry with you to defrost and eat cold or warm up for lunch in perfect portion sizes. **Canapés** will thrill all sorts of guests, from relatives during the holidays to game-day enthusiasts. **Mini Mains** are ideal for those nights you don't want to fuss and definitely don't want leftovers. **Sides and Dressings** are those little innovative touches that add pizzazz to other dishes. And **Sweets** need no explanation, especially if you've followed various websites and seen all those cute popsicle-stick goodies. But there aren't that many popsicle sticks in here, because I tried to give you recipes you wouldn't find anywhere else.

Within each chapter, you'll find 12 to 15 recipes for a range of ice cube tray shapes and sizes. They're designed to mix and match with each other so that you can do anything with them from keeping extra bounty from a garden to preparing a light meal for yourself or a companion to throwing a party filled with little, delicious bites, all prepared in ice cube trays.

When creating and testing these recipes, I used mostly common ingredients—there are only one or two that ask for luxury items like truffles—and techniques that most home cooks already know. (There are no sous vide recipes here!) For any items or methods that may be a little obscure, I've included explanations so you won't need to get on the Internet to figure it out. Also, keep in mind that all these trays are already nonstick, though in some cases, as my recipes direct, it doesn't hurt to also spray or brush them with cooking oil for ease of release.

I kept the instructions minimal and easy. The idea is to give you recipes that work but also inspire you to create your own. And part of the charm is in the exploration. Don't feel pressured to replicate them exactly. Instead, feel free to replace any of these ingredients with richer, more expensive, harder-to-find, more luxurious ones or to ramp up your technique. There's always more to imagine!

Caveats

Heat

When I began working with these ice cube trays, many of the manufacturers from whom I ordered claimed that they withstood temperatures from −40 to 446 degrees Fahrenheit (230 degrees Celsius). While I had no problems with the freezing, I did have some difficulties with the baking: all told, I melted a dozen trays. To avoid filling your house with that same distinct smell of burning plastic, I recommend not baking in any trays that are hard and seem inflexible, even if the manufacturer says it's okay. If there's any soft, pliable material in the bottom of the wells to help push out the ice cubes, those trays are great with frozen products or for making the Pear and Ricotta Mini Herbed Ravioli (see page 77), for example, but can't also be used with heat.

The best trays are the malleable, baking-grade silicone. If you can easily twist them with your hands and they spring back into shape, chances are you can bake with them and they won't melt. Some brands and shapes I counted on include:

- Webake (one-inch square, water bottle)
- Jacobake (mini spheres)
- IC ICLOVER (mini spheres)
- Heofean (mini grid)
- Big Chillers (two-inch cubes and squares)
- Adoric (two-inch cubes and squares)
- Cocktail Kingdom (two-inch square)
- KitchenHero (honeycomb)

However, the highest temperatures I subjected them to regularly was 375°F. I also don't recommend that you use them in a microwave oven—and be wary about using them to broil! I've used them in a convection gas oven as well as a regular gas oven, but again, make sure you're really only subjecting the true baking-grade silicone to these treatments.

Feel free to wash these in the dishwasher, though. I haven't melted one there yet! Like all plastic, the ice cube trays should only go in the top rack. Otherwise, you're risking prolonged exposure to hot water and steam.

Covers
Many of the trays come with covers, which is a bonus for when you want to freeze a recipe. The covers keep out odors from other items in the freezer, and they help with spillage. However, most don't fit well, so don't rely on them completely. I recommend that you cover trays with parchment or wax paper (you can use these interchangeably, although I call it parchment paper throughout the book) regardless of whether they have covers. If they do have covers, the parchment paper helps them fit more securely, and keeps the recipe from sticking. Don't use them for baking instead of foil or parchment paper. Some trays come with covers that pivot but aren't removable; these aren't helpful for baking.

Odors

Again, despite what manufacturers say, some of the trays arrive with an unpleasant smell. To rid them of it, soak them in a hot water-and-soap solution or run them through the dishwasher a couple times. That should do the trick.

After you use the ice cube trays with a pungent recipe—say, the frozen Pistachio-Arugula Pesto (see page 125), which contains raw garlic, or the refrigerated, molded The Coolest, Hottest Salsa (see page 53), which incorporates onion along with mango and pineapple—they may retain some of those aromas. Again, soak them in hot water and soap, or try not to let them sit in the freezer or refrigerator for too long before serving them. In cases of frozen items, once they're molded, you can remove them and keep them in plastic bags, and they'll retain their shapes.

Leftovers

Because some trays—especially the decorative ones—have odd measurements, or because you may not use the same trays that I did, the recipes may occasionally have some leftover parts or bits. The size of the eggs may also change your ratios. I used large eggs throughout. As you learn your trays, feel free to cut down or double recipes to achieve the best results.

Tools, Tips, and Techniques

Tools

You might think that the tools you need to make ice cube tray delicacies begin and end with the trays. As I experimented with various recipes and methodology for freezing, molding, and baking, I found that to be only partially true. As mentioned above, the ice cube trays come in a dizzying array of styles. Cooking in them, therefore, calls for a variety of techniques.

Tools you've find useful along the way include:

- Ice Cube Trays—If you're planning on creating your own recipes, the best thing to do first is to measure how much the ice cube tray holds. Just pour water into it from a measuring cup. Here's what I found from the ones I most commonly used:
    - Two-Inch Square, 6 wells = 3 cups, each well ½ cup
    - Two-Inch Sphere, 6 wells = 3 cups, each well ½ cup
    - One-Inch Square, 15 wells = 2 ½ cups
    - Mini Sphere, 20 wells = ½ cup
    - Mini Sphere, 36 wells = ¾ cup
    - Water Bottle, 4 wells = 1 cup
    - Water Bottle, 10 wells = ¾ cup

- Honeycomb, 37 wells = 1½ cups
- Baby Food, 9 wells = 3 cups, each well 1/3 cup
- Mini Grid, 160 wells = ¾ cup
- Layered, 8 wells = 2 cups, each well ¼ cup
- Decorative = ½ cup (fruit) to 1 cup (skulls) to 1½ cups (United States of America)

- Parchment/Wax Paper—Use to cover the trays, unmold food from trays, and knead dough
- Dropper—Depending on consistency of the recipe, use to fill the wells of the ice cube trays or remove too much liquid through suction
- Turkey Baster—Depending on consistency of the recipe, use to fill the wells of the ice cube trays or remove too much liquid through suction
- Piping Bag and Tips—Depending on consistency of the recipe, use to fill the wells of the ice cube trays
- Funnel—Depending on consistency of the recipe, use to fill the wells of the ice cube trays
- Spray Can—Use to mist cooking oil in the wells of trays
- Pastry Brush—Use to brush cooking oil onto the wells of the ice cube trays
- Cake Scraper—Use to clean the tops of the ice cube trays
- Mini Spatula—Use to loosen cooked food from the ice cube tray wells before unmolding
- Tongs—Use to remove cooked food from ice cube tray wells

Tips

In general, you can usually only purchase these ice cube trays online. Keep in mind that all the trays and their wells (sometimes called cavities, a word I chose not to use because it reminds me of the dentist) look bigger than they are in real life. It's easy to be fooled by the visuals versus the actual dimensions.

Additionally, as mentioned previously, not all the trays jibe with the manufacturers' instructions. When I came across those that were marketed inaccurately, I usually wrote to the manufacturers, asked them to correct information, and also asked for my money back. They all complied. If you wind up purchasing trays that don't do what they say they can do, don't hesitate to complain.

- Freezing
  - Some trays come with covers. They don't all fit well, but they're useful in keeping unpleasant freezer odors and/or flavors from contaminating the cubes.
  - If trays don't have covers, use plastic wrap or parchment/wax paper on top of forming cubes to keep them pure.

- Don't overfill the trays. Releasing overfilled trays can result in cracked ice, which will ruin your creations. Keep in mind that all liquid, but especially dairy, expands when freezing, so always underfill the wells just a bit. Underfill a little bit more when using liquids or semi-solids with dairy in them.
- When freezing sodas like cola, add diet soda to make harder ice cubes. Sugary liquids don't freeze as firmly as faux-sugar or non-sugar liquids and may stick to parchment paper. Use plastic wrap instead. Also, keep in mind you will mostly be left with the flavor, not the carbonation, of soda ice cubes. Unless the ice tray covers are absolutely airtight (and again, most of these covers are not), the carbon dioxide will dissipate.
- If any individual wells are overfull, you can use a dropper or turkey baster to easily extract liquid without having to dump the whole tray.
- Generally speaking, it takes about 6 hours for ice cubes to freeze solidly. Instructions often recommend that you leave ice sitting in trays overnight for best results. However, depending on the tray—and your freezer—your results may vary. I've achieved viable ice in as little as 3 hours with a side-by-side French door refrigerator with a bottom freezer, because the top shelf in this freezer is very cold. You can experiment and learn your fastest times, but overall, you should expect ice to take anywhere from 4 to 6 hours at the least.
- Baking
  - I can't say it enough: Be careful when choosing which trays to put into the oven. Not all are heat proof. Those that have extra material on the bottoms to "pop out" the ice cubes are generally not oven proof.
  - Bake at higher than 375°F at your own risk. Although the manufacturers will include instructions that food-grade silicone can withstand a range of temperatures from −40 (one or two say −50) to 464°F (230°C), some of these trays melt almost immediately when the oven gets too hot for extended periods of time.
  - Don't broil food in the trays for a long period of time. That's like pointing flames directly at them. It's risky. A few seconds for browning or melting might be okay. Use your judgment after you've used the trays a few times.
- Molding
  - Olive oil will freeze and can be used as a molding agent. It doesn't freeze clearly, however; instead, it becomes cloudy, opaque—more like butter. If you're planning to present your cubes, you may want to use gelatin instead.
  - Gelatin powder is the easiest way to mold items in trays. Follow the directions on the boxes of unflavored gelatin to prepare it before adding to recipes. Note:

Gelatin generally contains animal products and is not considered vegetarian or vegan. It also has a slight aroma but not a flavor.

- Pectin and agar are two vegan substances that can replace gelatin in recipes. Keep in mind that pectin requires sugar to gel, and agar might be harder to find in a general supermarket. Follow package directions for both if you replace gelatin with either substance.

- Unmolding
  - The silicone trays are made to twist easily and pop out the cubes, but they don't always readily pop out. Instead, lay a sheet of parchment paper on the counter. Turn the tray upside down, then twist. I like to hold them low and close to parchment paper. It catches cubes of all shapes and sizes so that they don't slide off the counter.
  - For molds and baked items, gently slide a thin, dull knife blade around the edges if they look like they won't unmold easily.

Techniques

- **Icing:** Thick liquids, cheeses, and batters can be difficult to get into the small wells of trays without making a mess. Like icing a cake, start filling the tray from the center and smooth outward until all the wells are filled. This can be done with a utensil like a spatula, a ladle, a knife, or sometimes, depending on the substance, your hands.
- **Dropping:** Thin liquids are sometimes best "dropped" into the wells with a dropper or a turkey baster.
- **Edging:** Use a cake scraper to clean the surfaces of the trays, so that you can present them without unmolding if you wish.

Infusions and Decorations

Solid Edible Petals

Ice Cube Tray: 1-Inch Square ⬭ Makes 15 cubes

Edible flowers are not only a beautiful way to garnish food and drinks; they also add a subtle tang. In fact, every flower has a different taste to it. When frozen in ice, they retain their freshness and flavor and make any drink look as if it were prepared by the most renowned mixologist. However, depending on where you live and what season it is, you may not be able to find fresh edible flowers. You can use dried flowers or flowers preserved in syrups, which make the ice just as pretty and flavorful, but in a slightly different manner.

1 handful washed edible petals, pistils and stamens removed

1 cup of your favorite spring water, still or sparkling

Lay out a 15-well, 1-inch square ice cube tray.

Divide petals evenly between wells. Fill the wells with the water, again dividing evenly. Be careful not to overfill, or ice cubes will be hard to release and may crack.

Place flat in freezer and cover with ice cube tray cover or parchment paper. Freeze for 4 to 6 hours before use. To unmold, crack the tray over parchment paper and serve in an ice bucket, glasses, or a punch bowl for best effect.

THINK OUTSIDE THE TRAY

Replace the water with a clear flavored beverage. Or squeeze lime, lemon, grapefruit, orange, or other citrus into the water first for a hint of sweet-tartness—not to mention vitamins.

EDIBLE FLOWERS

Many of us are familiar with a few edible flowers we often see garnishing restaurant dishes: zesty orange nasturtium, tart hibiscus, rose petals of various hues. But there are actually more than three dozen edible flowers—that is, if you're just counting flowers that bloom for their sake alone, and not those that presage fruits or vegetables or herbs. Add those in, and you have quite a fascinating list from which to choose. The blog *What's Cooking America* has a truly comprehensive list, along with some dos and don'ts to follow.

I Heart Jell-O Shots

Ice Cube Tray: Decorative 🧊 Makes 36 cubes

Unless you've been living under a rock—like literally, because you're a salamander—you've probably had a Jell-O shot or two. I don't know anyone of age who doesn't love them. This recipe is for adults, of course, but you can also leave out the alcohol and make fun molds with kids just because.

3–4 tablespoons minced strawberries

½ cup vodka

1½ cups water, divided

1 package strawberry Jell-O

Lay out three decorative hearts, shells, and stars ice cube trays.

In a pitcher, add the berries and vodka. Stir gently and leave to macerate.

Boil 1 cup of the water. Add the contents of the Jell-O. Stir until it is dissolved. Add the strawberry-vodka mix and the remaining ½ cup of cold water.

Use a dropper or turkey baster to fill the ice cube tray wells. Cover with parchment paper, and chill until molded, about 2 to 3 hours. To unmold, gently remove the shots with your fingers and serve on a tray.

THINK OUTSIDE THE TRAY

Try any combination of fruit and Jell-O. They don't have to match. Make a fruit cocktail!

Lots of Latte

Ice Cube Tray: Mini Grid 🎩 Makes 160 cubes

You know that cup or two of coffee that's always left in the pot? You come home from work and there it is, staring at you with its cold, dark gaze. Don't toss it down the drain. Instead, transform some of it into latte ice cubes. Then, pour the rest into a Mason jar, cover, and place in the refrigerator for up to two weeks. The next time you want a refreshing cup of iced java, you'll have both chilled coffee and frozen cubes that won't dilute it.

⅓ cup coffee (dark roast or espresso), hot or cold

⅔ cup milk of your choice, steamed or cold

Lay out a 160-well, mini grid ice cube tray.

In a bowl, combine the coffee and milk. Adjust until you achieve your desired coffee-to-milk ratio.

Using a dropper, fill ice cube tray wells with coffee mixture. Don't overfill or ice cubes will be hard to release.

Note: The mini ice cube tray holds about ¾ of a cup, so you will have a little bit of latte left over.

Cover with parchment paper and freeze until solid, about 3 to 4 hours. To unmold, crack the tray over parchment paper and serve in a glass pitcher.

THINK OUTSIDE THE TRAY

Turn latte cubes into Cuban café con leche cubes by adding demerara sugar (to taste) to the mixture. If you add the sugar to the coffee or to the milk while it's hot, it will dissolve.

Chai Tea

Ice Cube Tray: Mini Grid 🎩 Makes 320 cubes

Every chai tea recipe varies slightly, simply because it doesn't have just one point of origin. This recipe takes the middle road by using common spices, black tea, and almond milk, which blends with other substances better than dairy. For instance, you can make an awesome Arnold Palmer by adding these ice cubes to lemonade. Or use them in a cocktail. The cubes will increase the zest of whatever you're drinking as they melt.

1 cup water

1 cup almond milk

4 teaspoons loose black tea
(or 2 black tea bags)

1 piece fresh ginger, thumbnail size

1 cinnamon stick, lightly crushed

4 cloves, crushed

4 green cardamom pods, lightly crushed (substitute ½ teaspoon lightly crushed cardamom seeds)

4 black peppercorns, crushed

4 teaspoons sugar (or to taste)

Lay out a pair of 160-well, mini grid ice cube trays.

In an uncovered saucepan, combine all the ingredients except the sugar. Bring to a gentle boil, then reduce to a simmer. Allow to simmer for 10 to 15 minutes or until tea is very aromatic.

Remove from heat and drain through a fine-mesh strainer. Stir in the sugar while the fluid is still hot. Sweeten to taste.

Using a dropper, fill ice cube tray wells with tea mixture. Don't overfill or ice cubes will be hard to release.

Note: The mini ice cube tray holds about ¾ of a cup, so you will have a little bit of chai tea left over.

Cover with parchment paper and freeze until solid, about 3 to 4 hours. To unmold, crack the tray over parchment paper and serve in a glass pitcher.

THINK OUTSIDE THE TRAY

Try this with green or white tea instead of black tea for different flavor profiles. You can even brew it with rooibos.

Hot Chocolate Chunks
with Marshmallows

Ice Cube Tray: 1-Inch Square 🎩 Makes 15 cubes

Hot chocolate isn't just for the winter. Frozen hot chocolate is just as delectable! You can enjoy these cubes, which take their inspiration from Mexico, as miniature popsicles or pop a bunch of them into a blender and make a slushy to slurp on a summer's day.

2 cups milk

2 tablespoons baking cocoa

¼ cup sugar

½ teaspoon vanilla extract

½ teaspoon cinnamon

½ teaspoon chili powder

Pinch of salt

30 miniature marshmallows

Lay out a 15-well, 1-inch square ice cube tray.

In a saucepan over a low flame, combine all the ingredients except miniature marshmallows. Stir while heating until the cocoa, sugar, spices, and salt have all dissolved and mixture is hot.

Remove from heat and allow to cool completely. Using a dropper or turkey baster, fill the wells of the ice cube tray, filling each approximately ⅔ of the way.

Add 2 miniature marshmallows to the top of each well. They should float. Cover with parchment paper and freeze until solid, about 4 to 6 hours. To unmold, crack the tray over parchment paper and serve as a sorbet, or blend while still frozen to make a hot chocolate smoothie to drink.

THINK OUTSIDE THE TRAY

Add pizzazz to your hot chocolate by using flavored coffee creamers. You can make hazelnut, French vanilla, caramel macchiato—whatever flavor you like—simply by adding a couple of tablespoons to the recipe. You can also add flavored syrups like they do in coffee bars. Just remember to cut down the quantity of sugar that you use if you do so, as both creamers and syrups are very sweet.

Lavender Lemonade

Ice Cube Tray: Water Bottle 🜨 Makes 20 cubes

These clever ice cubes are excellent for inserting into water bottles, as they're designed to be. Add them to any water, seltzer, or juice to freshen the flavor of it. They're also wonderful to keep around for when you need a hit of citrus for a sweet recipe.

Juice of 2 lemons (substitute ¼ cup bottled juice)

2 cups spring water

½–1 cup Lavender Syrup (see recipe pg 22)

Lay out a pair of 10-well, water bottle ice cube trays.

In a pitcher, combine the lemon juice, water, and Lavender Syrup to taste. Pour into ice cube tray wells and freeze until solid, about 4 to 6 hours. To unmold, crack the tray over parchment paper and serve in a glass.

THINK OUTSIDE THE TRAY

Use any combination of citrus for tasty, refreshing ice cubes. Add some tangerine juice, or some grapefruit juice—whatever is fresh and in season. You can also switch out the herbs in the syrup. Try basil, sage, or thyme. Infused simple syrups are inexpensive and easy to make, a convenient way to preserve the fresh herbs of the season, and impressive to give as gifts. They also keep well in the refrigerator since sugar is a natural preservative.

HOW TO JUICE LEMONS

Here's how you can get the most juice out of your lemons: First, make sure to wash them. A lot of people skip this step, which is a mistake. All fruit is exposed to a variety of toxins, even if it's grown organically (remember, birds and squirrels live in trees, not mention a variety of insects), and what's on the outside can be transferred to the inside via a knife. Next, roll the lemons for a few minutes on a board or the countertop, pressing down on the fruit. Finally, if you're going to use the lemons to make lemonade, macerate the rinds with a little sugar—you'll be amazed how much more juice you draw out of the lemons this way.

Mojito Twizzles

Ice Cube Tray: Water Bottle 🎩 Makes 20 cubes

Straws are going the way of the dinosaur, and so are swizzle sticks. So why not simply stir your cocktail with a stick of flavored ice instead? Problem solved! And no waste involved.

Juice of 2 limes
   (or ¼ cup bottled juice)

2 cups seltzer water

½–1 cup Mint Syrup
   (see recipe page 22)

Lay out a pair of 10-well, water bottle ice cube trays.

In a pitcher, combine the lime juice, seltzer water, and Mint Syrup to taste. Pour into ice cube tray wells and freeze until solid, about 4 to 6 hours. To unmold, crack the tray over parchment paper and serve in a glass.

•⸱•⸱⸱•⸱•⸱⸱⸱⸱⸱•⸱•⸱⸱⸱•⸱⸱•⸱⸱⸱⸱⸱⸱⸱⸱⸱⸱•⸱•⸱⸱⸱⸱⸱⸱•⸱•⸱⸱⸱⸱•⸱⸱•

THINK OUTSIDE THE TRAY

If you like a touch of bitter flavors on your palate, replace the seltzer water with tonic. For extra freshness, use cucumber water!

Piña Colada Pineapples

Ice Cube Tray: Decorative 🎩 Makes about 12 cubes

You can make these little pineapple-based cuties with or without the rum. If you prefer to make them with, don't overdo it—too much booze could make them slushy.

¾ cup pineapple

2 tablespoons coconut cream

2 tablespoons white rum

Lay out a decorative pineapple ice cube tray.

In a blender or food processor, combine the pineapple, coconut cream, and rum. Pour or spoon the mixture into ice cube tray wells, cover with parchment paper, and freeze until solid, about 3 to 4 hours. To unmold, crack the tray over parchment paper and serve in a cocktail as a garnish.

THINK OUTSIDE THE TRAY

To add complexity to the concoction and lessen the acidity, try using grilled or roasted pineapple.

Margarita Cacti

Ice Cube Tray: Decorative 🎩 Makes 6 cubes

Hook these ice cubes as garnishes on your cocktail glasses for your next party—and don't be surprised when your guests post pictures of them on social media!

Juice of 4 limes (or ¼ cup bottled lime juice)

Zest of 1 lime

4 tablespoons tequila

2 tablespoons Simple Syrup (see recipe page 22)

Lay out a decorative cactus ice cube tray.

In a cocktail shaker, combine the lime, lime zest, tequila, and Simple Syrup. Use a dropper to fill the ice cube tray wells. Cover with parchment paper, and freeze until solid, about 3 to 4 hours. To unmold, crack the tray over parchment paper and serve in a cocktail as a garnish.

THINK OUTSIDE THE TRAY

To make these even more fun, stir together some kosher salt and sugar. Just before serving, dip the ice into the mixture so that the cubes sparkle and also get that telltale margarita flavor.

SIMPLE SYRUP VERSUS RICH SYRUP

Simple Syrup is not equivalent to sugar. In fact, it's a little less sweet. If you like your syrup more on the sweet side, make it Rich Syrup, where the ratio is not 1:1 sugar to water. Instead, it's 2:1 sugar to water. So just double the sugar. It will take a little longer to dissolve and have more "legs" in the container, meaning that it will cling to the sides more and look a bit thicker. And you can get away with using less of it. Rich Syrup also lasts longer. Store it in the refrigerator for up to 6 months.

Lavender Syrup

Makes 1½ cups

1 cup water

1 cup sugar

5–6 sprigs food-grade lavender

In a small saucepan, bring the water to a boil. Add the sugar and whisk or stir it until it dissolves.

Add the lavender and boil for 1 minute, then remove from heat. Allow to steep for 30 minutes.

Remove the lavender and strain the syrup through a fine-mesh strainer into a container with a lid. Store in the refrigerator for up to one month.

Mint Syrup

Makes 1½ cups

1 cup water

1 cup sugar

5–6 sprigs fresh mint

In a small saucepan, bring the water to a boil. Add the sugar and whisk or stir it until it dissolves.

Add the mint and boil for 1 minute, then remove from heat. Allow to steep for 30 minutes.

Remove the mint and strain the syrup through a fine-mesh strainer into a container with a lid. Store in the refrigerator for up to one month.

Simple Syrup

Makes 1½ cups

1 cup water

1 cup sugar

In a small saucepan, combine water and sugar. Heat over a medium flame, stirring until the sugar is dissolved. Remove from heat and pour into a container with a lid. Refrigerate until and after use. Simple syrup keeps in the refrigerator for about a month.

White Sangria Stars

Ice Cube Tray: Decorative 🎩 Makes about 12 cubes

By using white wine to make these ice cubes, you can see all the ingredients that comprise them. They look gorgeous floating in a glass of wine—or, of course, more sangria.

½ green or red apple, finely diced

6 green or red table grapes, quartered

1 cup white wine

1 tablespoon brandy

1 tablespoon fresh lemon juice

1 tablespoon orange zest

2 tablespoons Simple Syrup (see recipe page 22)

Lay out a decorative stars ice cube tray.

Divide the apple and grapes evenly among the wells.

In a cocktail shaker, combine the wine, brandy, lemon juice, orange zest, and Simple Syrup. Use a dropper or turkey baster to fill the ice cube tray wells. Cover with parchment paper and freeze until solid, about 3 to 4 hours. To unmold, crack the tray over parchment paper and serve in a glass, pitcher, or punch bowl as a garnish.

THINK OUTSIDE THE TRAY

Sangria is also enjoyable if you use strawberries and mango, especially with white wine—the mango brings out the tropical notes in certain varietals. In fact, you can use any fruit you have on hand and any hue of wine.

Cherry Cola Squares

Ice Cube Tray: 1-Inch Square 🎩 Makes 15 cubes

This recipe is a wonderful way to preserve fruit from the brief summer cherry season, when flavors are at their peak. However, you can also use whole frozen cherries when they're not in season; they work just as well. Either way, we like to use these ice cubes in cocktails—the cherry cola flavor is ideal in an aged rum with a fine bourbon poured over it and a lemon peel garnish. As the ice melts, the drink slowly transforms, so you get a different flavor profile with every sip.

2 tablespoons grenadine

2 tablespoons maraschino cherry syrup

1 cup cola

1 cup diet cola

15 whole cherries, either fresh with pits and stems intact or frozen

Lay out a 15-well, 1-inch square ice cube tray.

In a small pitcher, combine the grenadine, maraschino cherry syrup, and cola. Stir gently; you don't want to flatten the soda completely. Pouring carefully, divide liquid between the wells of the ice cube tray until each is about ⅔ of the way full.

Add the whole cherries, one each to a well. If wells are too full, use a dropper to extract liquid.

Place the tray in the freezer. Cover lightly with plastic wrap (if desired) and freeze until solid, about 4 to 6 hours. To unmold, crack the tray over parchment paper and serve in a cocktail.

THINK OUTSIDE THE TRAY

If you have the availability, try this with different varieties and colors of cherries that are on the market: Bing, Chelan, Lambert, Montmorency, Rainier, Queen Anne, and more. You can also change the soda. Cream soda is striking, too. Or replace the grenadine and maraschino cherry syrup with ½ teaspoon of sugar and a couple of dashes of bitters. Voilà! You'll have a cherry old-fashioned ice cube for your whiskey. Add vermouth and make it a Manhattan.

Red-and-Blue Berry Sparklers

Ice Cube Tray: Decorative 🎩 Makes 48 cubes (mainland only)

This patriotic ice cube tray is adorable for Fourth of July parties and picnics. It's truly impressive if you can use the berries correctly in the red and blue states. But I found the ice cube wells are a little small for such geographical accuracy—and I prefer unity, anyway.

3–4 tablespoons minced strawberries and/or raspberries

3–4 tablespoons minced blueberries and/or blackberries

1 cup lemon-lime soda

Lay out a decorative United States of America ice cube tray.

In a pitcher, add the berries and soda. Stir gently.

Use a dropper or turkey baster to fill the ice cube tray wells. Cover with plastic wrap—parchment paper sometimes sticks to the tops of the berries if they float up—and freeze until solid, about 4 to 6 hours. To unmold, crack the tray over parchment paper and serve in glasses.

THINK OUTSIDE THE TRAY

If you really want to go all out for the Fourth of July, leave out the berries and grab some food coloring. It takes a steady hand with a dropper, but you can certainly try for some tie-dye or red-white-and-blue state ice cubes.

Soups and Smoothies

Chunky Gazpacho

Ice Cube Tray: Baby Food 🧊 Makes 9 baby food cups

Nothing is more refreshing than a chilled cup of gazpacho. The gazpacho is a helpful way to preserve tomatoes at the height of their summer ripeness. Don't limit yourself to the usual red tomatoes, either. This can be made with yellow, orange, or any heirloom tomato on the market.

1 cup peeled, seeded, and chopped tomatoes

1 clove garlic, minced

¼ cup finely chopped English cucumber

¼ cup finely chopped red onion

¼ cup finely chopped green bell pepper

1 tablespoon minced basil

½ teaspoon ground cumin

½ teaspoon paprika

Freshly ground salt and black pepper to taste

1 tablespoon fresh lime juice

1 tablespoon balsamic vinegar

1 teaspoon Worcestershire sauce

¼ cup olive oil

1 cup tomato juice

Lay out a 9-well, baby food ice cube tray.

In a bowl, combine the tomatoes, garlic, cucumber, onion, bell pepper, basil, cumin, paprika, and salt and pepper. Mix well and allow to sit.

In a food processor or blender, combine the lime juice, balsamic vinegar, Worcestershire sauce, olive oil, and tomato juice. Blend well.

Spoon ⅓ of the tomato mixture into the tomato liquid and blend again until puréed.

Pour the tomato purée over the chopped tomato mixture and stir to combine. Divide evenly between ice cube tray wells, cover with parchment paper or lid, and freeze until solid, about 4 to 6 hours. To serve, unmold, place in a bowl and allow the cubes to defrost, or serve frozen as a palate-cleansing sorbet.

THINK OUTSIDE THE TRAY

Replace the tomatoes and tomato juice with fruit! Watermelon makes an excellent gazpacho, as does mango. Strawberry does, too. Try different combinations, both with and without tomatoes. There's no limit with inventing riffs on gazpacho!

HOW TO PEEL TOMATOES

Prepare a pot of boiling water and an ice bath. On the bottom of each tomato, cut an X into the skin. Drop the tomatoes into boiling water for 10 to 15 seconds, then transfer to the ice bath. The skin will start to curl up, and you can slide it right off. Then core the tomatoes and seed them before use.

LOOKING AHEAD . . . FIVE FACTS ABOUT VICHYSSOISE (PAGE 33)

1. It was invented in 1917 at the Ritz-Carlton Hotel in New York.

2. Although it was created in America, the culinary mastermind behind it was French. Louis Diat modeled it after the potato-leek soup popular in his home country.

3. Diat originally called it Crème Vichyssoise Glacée, named for his town of Vichy.

4. He made it for the opening of the rooftop garden of the Ritz, which is why it had to be served cold.

5. Vichyssoise doesn't have to be eaten cold, however, and is just as mouthwatering when served hot.

Baby Potato Vichyssoise

Ice Cube Tray: Baby Food 🎩 Makes 9 baby food cups

Vichyssoise may be thought of as a "cold soup," but it's actually best served at room temperature. If you're going to bring a container of frozen vichyssoise to work with you or on a picnic, it's a good idea to transfer it to the refrigerator the night before so that it begins to acclimate slowly to a higher temperature. Then, the next day, it will have less of a thaw to perform.

1 tablespoon butter

1 tablespoon olive oil

½ white onion

2 leeks, white and green parts, sliced

1 cup chopped baby potatoes, skin on

Freshly ground sea salt and white pepper to taste

2 cups chicken stock

¼ cup heavy cream

½ teaspoon nutmeg

1 teaspoon chopped fresh chives

Lay out a 9-well, baby food ice cube tray.

In a heavy saucepot, melt the butter with the olive oil over medium heat. Add the onion and sweat until translucent. Add the leek and stir to combine. Cook until soft, about 4 to 5 minutes.

Add the potatoes to the pot and stir. Cook for 2 to 3 minutes, then season with salt and pepper. Stir. Add the chicken stock. Reduce heat to low and cook at a simmer until potatoes can be pierced with a fork, about 20 to 25 minutes.

In a blender or using a hand blender, purée the soup. Add the cream and nutmeg. Cook for 5 more minutes. Remove from heat and allow to cool completely.

Divide evenly between ice cube tray wells and garnish with chives. Cover with parchment paper or lid, and freeze until solid, about 4 to 6 hours.

Note: Don't fill cups up to the top. Dairy expands when frozen, so leave a little room. You will likely have some soup left over—enjoy a serving while it's hot! To serve, unmold, place in a bowl and allow the cubes to defrost.

THINK OUTSIDE THE TRAY

Give vichyssoise even more international flair by incorporating sweet potatoes, yuca (cassava), taro root, malanga, or boniato. While all these roots have slightly different flavors, they are all mildly sweet with a high starch content, and that's what's important here.

Cucumber-Avocado
with Goat Cheese Crumbles

Ice Cube Tray: Baby Food 🍶 Makes 9 baby food cups

This tangy, refreshing cold soup is ideal during summer, but also a perfect winter's pick-me-up when the heater is going full blast and your skin feels dry and in need of vitamins and oils. The good fats in the avocado and yogurt, plus the water in the cucumber, supply plenty of thirst-quenching nutrients.

½ cup puréed cucumber, drained

1 cup puréed avocado

½ cup yogurt, drained

1 tablespoon white vinegar

1 tablespoon fresh lime juice

1 tablespoon minced scallions

1 teaspoon minced fresh sage

1 teaspoon minced fresh oregano

Freshly ground sea salt and white pepper to taste

½ cup goat cheese crumbles

Lay out a 9-well, baby food ice cube tray.

In a food processor, combine all the ingredients except for the goat cheese and blend thoroughly. Fold in goat cheese crumbles.

Dividing evenly, fill wells ⅔ of the way. This soup will expand when it freezes. Cover and freeze, about 4 to 6 hours. To serve, unmold, place in a bowl, and allow the cubes to defrost, or blend as a smoothie while still frozen to drink.

THINK OUTSIDE THE TRAY

Change the cheese. Several cheeses freeze well, including feta, which will add a Greek flair; Mexican queso fresco; and Stilton, which is the most pungent of the three mentioned here. Adjust the herbs to match the nationality of your soup, and you can have a different recipe each time.

A Better Borscht

Ice Cube Tray: Baby Food 🎩 Makes 9 baby food cups

Borscht is an old-fashioned and gag-producing concoction your grandma used to make, right? Not this version, which is vegetarian and adds apples to the beets and cabbage. Sweet and tart by turns, with a stunning scarlet hue, this recipe can be savored as a soup or a smoothie at any time of the day.

2 tablespoons vegetable oil

½ onion, chopped

1 clove garlic, minced

1 stalk celery, chopped

1 carrot, chopped

1 apple, cored and finely chopped

1 cup finely chopped fresh beets

½ cup shredded white cabbage

1 tablespoon tomato paste

1 tablespoon fresh dill

½ teaspoon allspice

Freshly ground sea salt and black pepper to taste

1½ cups vegetable stock

1 bay leaf

2 tablespoons red wine vinegar

1 cup sour cream for serving (optional)

Lay out a 9-well, baby food ice cube tray.

In a stockpot, add oil over a medium flame. When hot, add onions, garlic, celery, and carrot. Sauté the mixture until the onions are translucent.

Add the apple, beets, and cabbage. Stir for 2 to 3 minutes until well incorporated. Add the tomato paste, dill, and allspice. Stir for another 2 to 3 minutes.

Cover the mixture with the stock and add the bay leaf. Add water if you need more liquid to cover the vegetables. Bring to a boil, then reduce to a simmer. Cook for 30 minutes or until all ingredients are fork tender.

Remove from heat. Stir in red wine vinegar and allow to cool. Remove bay leaf.

Dividing evenly, fill the wells. Cover and freeze, about 4 to 6 hours. To serve, unmold, place in a bowl, and allow the cubes to defrost. Add a dollop of sour cream if desired, or blend with sour cream as a smoothie while still frozen to drink.

THINK OUTSIDE THE TRAY

For more traditional borscht, use beef broth instead of vegetable broth and leave out the apple.

Zesty Carrot-Parsnip

Ice Cube Tray: Baby Food 🧊 Makes 9 baby food cups

The carrots and parsnips, together with the nutmeg, make this sweet-tasting but piquant cold soup a natural for fall lunches. But it can also be served hot. Make a double or triple batch and serve it for dinner, then freeze the rest for another time.

2 tablespoons vegetable oil

½ onion, chopped

1 clove garlic, minced

1 stalk celery, chopped

1 potato, peeled and chopped

½ cup chopped carrots

½ cup chopped parsnips

¼ teaspoon nutmeg

½ teaspoon cumin

1 teaspoon chili powder

1 teaspoon paprika

1 teaspoon cayenne pepper

Freshly ground sea salt and black pepper to taste

1½ cups vegetable stock

1 bay leaf

¼ cup cream

Lay out a 9-well, baby food ice cube tray.

In a stockpot, add oil over a medium flame. When hot, add onions, garlic, celery, potato, carrots, and parsnips. Sauté the mixture until the onions are translucent. Add the cumin, chili powder, paprika, cayenne pepper, and salt and pepper. Stir to coat.

Cover the mixture with the stock and add the bay leaf and nutmeg. Add water if you need more liquid to cover the vegetables. Bring to a boil, then reduce to a simmer. Cook for 30 minutes or until all ingredients are fork tender.

Remove from heat. Allow to cool. When warm, stir in the cream. Remove bay leaf.

Dividing evenly, fill the wells ⅔ of the way. This soup will expand when it freezes. Cover and freeze, about 4 to 6 hours. To serve, unmold, place in a bowl, and allow the cubes to defrost.

THINK OUTSIDE THE TRAY

Other root vegetables will add a variety of flavor profiles to this soup. Turnips make a terrific addition. Starchier roots like yuca, boniato, or sweet potatoes can substitute for the potatoes.

Strawberry Coconut Cream

Ice Cube Tray: Baby Food ⬭ Makes 9 baby food cups

The addition of balsamic vinegar in this recipe deepens the strawberry flavor, and the use of coconut milk keeps it lactose free.

2 cups roughly chopped strawberries, divided

1 tablespoon balsamic vinegar

2 tablespoons sugar

1 cup coconut milk

¼ cup coconut cream

2 tablespoons julienne fresh basil

Lemon wedges for serving (optional)

Lay out a 9-well, baby food ice cube tray.

In a bowl, mix the strawberries, balsamic vinegar, and sugar together. Allow the berries to macerate for about 5 minutes.

In a food processor, blend 1½ cups of the berries, coconut milk, coconut cream, and basil until smooth. Return the purée to the bowl with the remaining ½ cup of berries and fold gently together.

Dividing evenly, fill the wells of the ice cube tray with the basil, then the berry mixture. Cover and freeze, about 4 to 6 hours. To serve, unmold, place in a bowl, and allow the cubes to defrost, or serve frozen as a sorbet. Garnish with a wedge of sugared lemon (optional) or blend with lemon while still frozen as a smoothie to drink.

THINK OUTSIDE THE TRAY

Try other non-dairy milks, pastes, and butters in place of coconut to vary the flavor and texture. Almond milk and almond butter also work beautifully, lending it a significantly different profile. You can use soy milk, too. You may have to play around with the amounts of each and sugar levels depending on what you choose, however.

Minty Melon Heaven

Ice Cube Tray: 1-Inch Square 🎩 Makes 15 cubes

Borrowing elements from the mojito, this super-simple soup/smoothie offers a little sparkle to brighten your day. The tonic keeps it from becoming too sweet.

1⅔ cups roughly chopped honeydew melon

1 tablespoon fresh lime juice

1 teaspoon agave nectar

½ cup tonic

9 sprigs fresh mint (add more to taste)

Lay out a 15-well, 1-inch square ice cube tray.

In a food processor, blend all of the ingredients together.

Dividing evenly, fill the wells of the ice cube tray. Cover with parchment and freeze, about 4 to 6 hours. To serve, unmold, place in a bowl, and allow the cubes to defrost, or blend as a smoothie while still frozen to drink.

THINK OUTSIDE THE TRAY

This is a great soup/smoothie to explore the world of melons! Swap out the honeydew for any sweet melon: cantaloupe, Canary, Crenshaw, Sharlyn, or even red or yellow watermelon. These will all affect the sugar content, so try the flesh of the melon first, then experiment with the agave nectar ratio (more for cantaloupe, for example, less for watermelon). Or try a melon from a specialty market that you've never had before, like the Chinese Hami, the French Charentais, the Persian muskmelon, or the Israeli Galia.

Green All Day

Ice Cube Tray: 1-Inch Square 🧊 Makes 15 cubes

I admit it: I don't like kale. So this is a kale-free smoothie. In fact, this book is a kale-free zone. My dislike stems from my participation in a Community-Supported Agriculture group. For a decade, I hosted it, and no one ever took home their huge bunches of kale. I'd be left with so many pounds of the stuff that we'd be stewing it, dehydrating it, freezing it, and generally chewing on kale all week, all season long. After I quit the group, kale chips, kale Caesar salads, and kale smoothies came into fashion. Suddenly kale was everywhere and everything. The gall! I ate so much kale then, I can't even look at it now. It's all about spinach for me.

1 cup packed spinach (or ½ cup spinach and ½ cup arugula)

1 green apple, cored and chopped

1 small bunch parsley

1 thumb-sized piece fresh ginger

1 tablespoon lemon juice

1 teaspoon honey

1 cup white grape juice

Lay out a 15-well, 1-inch square ice cube tray.

In a food processor or high-powered blender, purée all the ingredients together.

Dividing evenly, fill the wells of the ice cube tray. Cover with parchment and freeze, about 4 to 6 hours. To serve, unmold, place in a food processor or blender, and blend while still frozen. Pour in a glass to drink.

THINK OUTSIDE THE TRAY

If you prefer a creamier green smoothie, replace the apple with banana. You can also use a ripe mango if available, which has such a high water content that you can cut the grape juice in half. Or replace the grape juice with mango juice, which adds a sweet, tropical flair to the smoothie.

Gingery Golden Apple

Ice Cube Tray: 1-Inch Square 🎩 Makes 15 cubes

You can leave the skin on the apples here or remove it—it's up to you. Just make sure you use a high-powered blender to eviscerate the apple flesh or this will be grainy.

1⅔ cups roughly chopped Golden Delicious and Granny Smith apple

¼ teaspoon nutmeg

1 teaspoon ground ginger

¼ teaspoon allspice

¼ teaspoon cinnamon

1 tablespoon fresh lemon juice

1 teaspoon honey

½ cup pear juice

Lay out a 15-well, 1-inch square ice cube tray.

In a bowl, mix the apples, spices, lemon juice, and honey together. Allow the apples to macerate for about 5 minutes.

In a food processor or high-powered blender, purée the apples and pear juice together.

Dividing evenly, fill the wells of the ice cube tray. Cover with parchment and freeze, about 4 to 6 hours. To serve, unmold, place in a food processor or blender, and blend while still frozen. Pour in a glass to drink.

THINK OUTSIDE THE TRAY

Pear juice is sweet but neutral and is an easy way to add moisture while allowing your smoothie to taste like the main ingredients. But if you want to add other flavors with your liquid, browse the refrigerated juices shelf of your local supermarket. You'll find everything from orange-banana to cold-pressed green juices that add pizzazz to homemade mixes.

Pineapple-Grapefruit
with Habanero and Basil

Ice Cube Tray: 1-Inch Square 🎩 Makes 15 cubes

My favorite juice when I was a child, long before cold-presses were a thing or before flavored mixtures were in the markets, there was this tart combo of pineapple and grapefruit. This amalgam was helped along, in part, by the service project that I had to participate in every fall: selling boxes of fresh citrus from Florida to fund various school band and orchestra activities. My mom always bought so many cases of grapefruit, which we stored in our freezing cold garage in New Jersey, that I was able to drink this all winter. These days, I like it to linger on the palate with heat and herbs.

1 cup roughly chopped pineapple

1 cup freshly squeezed grapefruit juice with pulp

½ habanero, with or without seeds

6 sprigs fresh basil

Lay out a 15-well, 1-inch square ice cube tray.

In a food processor or high-powered blender, purée all the ingredients together.

Dividing evenly, fill the wells of the ice cube tray. Cover with parchment and freeze, about 4 to 6 hours. To serve, unmold, place in a food processor or blender, and blend while still frozen. Pour in a glass to drink.

THINK OUTSIDE THE TRAY

Now that I live in Florida, I know how much more specialized the industry is beyond Navel orange and Ruby Red grapefruit. There's Hamlin, Temple, and Valencia oranges; Honey, Clementine, and Mandarin tangerines; and HoneyBell tangelos (a particularly popular hybrid of a tangerine and grapefruit). Florida also grows ortaniques, yuzus, and pomelos. Explore and enjoy them in this smoothie!

Good Morning, Mary

Ice Cube Tray: 1-Inch Square 🎩 Makes 15 cubes

The surprise additions of green olives and horseradish in this perky smoothie turn it into a lip-smacking breakfast cocktail. You'll be eager to start your day with this in your freezer!

1½ cups chopped tomatoes

¼ cup chopped celery

¼ cup fresh spinach

¼ Spanish green olives with pimentos, drained

1 tablespoon grated horseradish

1 tablespoon fresh lemon juice

1 teaspoon Worcestershire sauce

½ teaspoon Tabasco sauce

¼–½ cup ice

Freshly ground sea salt and black pepper to taste

Lay out a 15-well, 1-inch square ice cube tray.

In a blender, combine all the ingredients. Blend on high speed until frothy. If too thick, add more ice. Allow to settle, then divide evenly between the wells. Cover with parchment and freeze until solid, about 4 to 6 hours. To serve, unmold, place in a food processor or blender, and blend while still frozen. Pour in a glass to drink.

THINK OUTSIDE THE TRAY

For different flavor profiles, trade out the greens—arugula for the spinach, or baby spring leaves. Dandelion leaves! Anything tender will do. Even, if you prefer, the k-word (remember Green All Day? See page 43).

Banana Nut Bread

Ice Cube Tray: 1-Inch Square 🎩 Makes 15 cubes

This is my favorite smoothie, because it really does taste like banana nut muffins to me. The combination of walnuts, brown sugar, vanilla extract, and bananas is a win-win-win. Use a high-powered blender here so that the nuts don't make the mixture grainy. Sure, this one is a little on the sweet side, and it won't win the smoothie beauty pageant. But I've got no problem with that.

2 bananas

¼ cup unsalted walnuts

2 tablespoons brown sugar

1 teaspoon vanilla extract

1 cup milk

Lay out a 15-well, 1-inch square ice cube tray.

In a food processor or high-powered blender, purée all the ingredients together.

Dividing evenly, fill wells ⅔ of the way. This smoothie will expand as it freezes. Cover with parchment and freeze, about 4 to 6 hours. To serve, unmold, place in a food processor or blender, and blend while still frozen. Pour in a glass to drink.

THINK OUTSIDE THE TRAY

Make it strawberry-banana nut bread by adding a handful of ripe berries. Change the nuts to macadamias or almonds. Spice it up with a dash of cinnamon. You can also substitute maple syrup for the vanilla extract. This recipe is easy to switch up according to your preferences.

Canapés

The Coolest, Hottest Salsa

Ice Cube Tray: Honeycomb 🎩 Makes 37 cubes

This salsa is one of my favorites to make, not only because I have so many mango trees in my Miami backyard, but because the golden color looks so gorgeous in the jar. It's also a delightful, sweet-sour salsa to serve with fish or chicken as well as eat with chips. The pineapple adds tartness and the cucumber a clean liveliness, both counterpoints to super-sweet Florida mango. I like to let the ingredients mingle together for an hour or two before adding the gelatin and putting into the trays to mold.

½ ripe but firm mango, finely diced

¼ quarter cup finely diced fresh pineapple

½ small Vidalia onion, minced

½ cup English cucumber, finely diced

1 jalapeño, minced (use without seeds for less heat)

2 tablespoons fresh cilantro leaves, chopped

2 tablespoons fresh lime juice

Freshly ground sea salt and black pepper to taste

1 envelope powdered gelatin

Lay out a 37-well, honeycomb ice cube tray (or several decorative trays, as seen in photo).

Mix all ingredients except the gelatin in a non-reactive bowl. Allow to stand at room temperature for an hour or two for flavors to come together.

Dissolve one packet of gelatin in a cup of hot water. Add to the mango mixture and stir well.

Spoon the mango mixture into the wells. Cover with parchment paper and refrigerate for 24 hours. Unmold by removing the gelatin carefully with your fingers and serve with chips.

Note: These will melt quickly in the heat, so if you're planning on serving outside, pop them into the freezer for an hour.

THINK OUTSIDE THE TRAY

Use different chili peppers for a variety of explosive heat. Scotch bonnet peppers and bird peppers are two of the hottest ones you can easily find in markets, so if you really like spice, go for those. If you want to lend a smoky flavor to the salsa, roast the pepper first over a flame until the skin blackens, then peel it and add the flesh and seeds.

Salmon Terrine

Ice Cube Tray: 2-Inch Square 🧊 Makes 12 terrines

Making salmon terrine might leave your hands smelling a little fishy. Trust me, it's worth it. To clean up, just rub lemon over your palms and fingers, and don't go near any house cats with sharp teeth.

½ pound (8 ounces) cream cheese

¼ pound (4 ounces) smoked salmon

2 ounces crème fraîche

1 shallot, minced

2 tablespoons minced scallions

¼ cup minced celery

1 tablespoon minced capers

1 tablespoon minced dill

1 tablespoon fresh lemon juice

Freshly ground sea salt and black pepper to taste

12 slices of thinly sliced lox, gravlax, or Nova

Thin slices of English cucumber for garnish

Thin slices of lemon for garnish

Lay out a pair of 6-well, 2-inch square ice cube trays. Spray or brush them with cooking oil.

In a bowl, place the cream cheese, ¼ pound of salmon, crème fraîche, shallot, scallions, celery, capers, dill, lemon juice, and salt and pepper. Mix well until combined.

Shape some of the salmon filling, about the size and shape of a well, in the palm of your hand. Wrap it in a half piece of salmon to cover two sides. Turn and wrap another piece of salmon around the parts that are uncovered. It should now look like a square wrapped in salmon. Squeeze lightly to make sure there are no air pockets between the filling and the sliced salmon. Deposit it in a well; it should fit perfectly. Repeat until all wells are filled.

Cover the trays with parchment paper, then foil. Stack and weight them so that they settle as they mold. Refrigerate for at least 4 hours.

Slide a dull knife blade around the edges to loosen them. Unmold carefully with a mini spatula. Serve with pita or bagel chips and cucumber and lemon slices.

THINK OUTSIDE THE TRAY

While salmon is the one of the few oily, thinly sliced fishes you can easily find to use for the exterior, you can substitute any smoked fish for the interior. I've used whitefish, mackerel, and trout, and depending on where you live, you can likely find species near you that are native and plentiful. Tuna also is a meaty filling, as is sturgeon, bluefish, mullet, and marlin or sailfish.

Corned Beef Mash

Ice Cube Tray: 2-Inch Sphere 🎩 Makes 24 pancakes

This dish combines two favorite foods—corned beef hash and mashed potatoes. A marvelous way to use up leftovers! The pancakes have a soft interior studded with salty nuggets of corned beef. So the texture varies throughout, but you get that unmistakable taste of hash.

2 tablespoons butter

½ onion, chopped

½ bell pepper, chopped

1½ cups mashed potatoes

1 egg

1 cup chopped corn beef

½ teaspoon paprika

Freshly ground sea salt and black pepper to taste

Lay out a pair of 6-well, 2-inch sphere trays. Spray or brush with cooking oil.

Preheat the oven to 350°F.

In a pan, melt the butter over a medium flame. Sauté the onion and pepper until the onion is translucent. Remove from the heat and set aside.

In a bowl, place the mashed potatoes. Add the egg, the corned beef, and the onion-pepper mixture. Season with paprika, salt, and pepper. Combine well and form 24 pancakes the size and shape of the wells. Place 12 in the wells.

Place in the oven and bake until the pancakes turn crisp and golden brown, about 25 to 30 minutes. Remove from the oven and place pancakes on a paper towel to drain. Repeat the baking process with the remaining 12 pancakes. Serve on a platter as appetizers or plate several together as a starter with deli mustard.

THINK OUTSIDE THE TRAY

If you don't have corned beef on hand, mince leftovers from a roast, a steak, or a chop. Any beef, pork, lamb, or even poultry will work. Sweet potatoes can also substitute for white potatoes. In fact, they give the pancakes a lovely profile—especially if you combine them with leftover turkey.

Oven-Fried Zucchini Sticks

Ice Cube Tray: Water Bottle 🧊 Makes 12 sticks

It's almost impossible not to love fried zucchini, but it is possible to disdain the oil that often drips from it. This super simple recipe allows you to bake it instead, achieving similar results with half the calories and none of the grease. You can use any of the sauces in this book as dips, too; I recommend either a simple marinara (because who doesn't love that?) or the Sundried Tomato Sauce that pairs with the Mozzarella-Stuffed Meatballs (see page 98 for the recipe).

1 large zucchini, cut into thirds

2 eggs

1 tablespoon water

2 tablespoons flour

Freshly ground sea salt and black pepper to taste

1 cup plain or seasoned bread crumbs

1 tablespoon minced oregano

¼ cup grated Parmesan (optional)

Lay out a trio of 4-well, water bottle trays.

Preheat the oven to 350°F.

Cut each zucchini third into 4 sticks.

In a bowl, beat the eggs with the water.

In another bowl or plate big enough to dredge the zucchini sticks, mix the flour with the salt and pepper.

In a third bowl or plate, mix the bread crumbs with the oregano, more salt and pepper, and Parmesan.

Dredge a zucchini stick first in egg, then in the flour mixture, then back in the egg, then in the bread-crumb mixture. Place in an ice cube tray well. Repeat until all zucchini sticks have been coated.

Place in the oven and bake for 20 to 25 minutes or until the coating is golden brown and the zucchini is cooked through. Remove from the ice cube trays with tongs or a serving utensil. Serve immediately with dipping sauce.

THINK OUTSIDE THE TRAY

Summer squash will substitute for the zucchini, as will firmer vegetables such as jicama (no, really, try it). You can also cut long strips from large Portobello caps, or coat asparagus spears in the bread crumbs.

Baked Brie Pockets

Ice Cube Tray: 2-Inch Sphere 🎩 Makes 12 Brie pockets

The invention of miniature Brie rounds, which come in little containers or wraps that you eat whole, rind and all, has made this recipe almost ridiculously easy. Add a thawed sheet of puff pastry dough and you've got two out of three ingredients that you need. A condiment is the fun mystery ingredient. Read on to learn how to make it tropical!

2 sheets frozen puff pastry dough, thawed

12 quarter-inch cubes guava paste

½ cup macadamia nuts, lightly crushed

12 miniature Brie rounds

1 egg, beaten

Lay out a pair of 6-well, 2-inch sphere ice cube trays.

Preheat the oven to 350°F.

Roll out the puff pastry dough (see sidebar for How to Work with Puff Pastry) large enough to cut a dozen 2-inch diameter circles from each sheet. Using a biscuit or cookie cutter, cut 24 circles from the sheets.

Lay a circle of dough on parchment paper. In the center, place a guava square. Sprinkle it with macadamia nuts. Place a miniature Brie round on top and press down lightly. Top with a second pastry round and crimp the edges to seal. Brush both sides lightly with egg and place it in a well of the ice cube tray. Repeat until all the wells are filled.

Place in the oven and bake for 20 to 25 minutes or until the pastry is golden brown and the cheese is just starting to ooze out. To unmold, slide out with a mini spatula. Serve on a platter or place on a cheese tray.

THINK OUTSIDE THE TRAY

Replace the guava paste with quince paste. Or choose any mostardo or jam that you prefer. You can also switch up the nuts and try almonds, cashews, pecans, or walnuts. And champagne or honey mustard—or even honey itself—is a wonderful option bubbling up with the Brie, too.

(continued on next page)

HOW TO WORK WITH PUFF PASTRY

Puff pastry is a layered dough that you can—and should, given the time it takes to make it—buy frozen. It's called "puff pastry" because hot air gets into the dozens of layers when it bakes and the steam puffs it up. It usually comes in sheets, shells, or cups, and you can find it in the freezer section of your grocery store.

To work with puff pastry, always defrost it first. It can thaw in your refrigerator overnight before you use it for a recipe, or on your counter for 30 to 45 minutes. After that, it's very pliable. You can roll out the sheets and cut them into any shapes that you desire.

Puff pastry is ideal for making ice cube tray recipes because it's both neutral—you can use it for sweet or savory dishes—and flexible. And if it tears, you can repair it by smoothing it over with a little water to fix the dough.

To bake puff pastry, always preheat the oven. Dark trays will cook it faster, and an egg wash will turn it golden brown.

Toasted Garlic Non-"Naan"

Ice Cube Tray: 2-Inch Sphere ⬭ Makes 24–36 flatbreads

Because this flatbread is baked in an ice cube tray and not in a clay oven, it's not exactly naan. But it does have some elements of that fabulous Indian bread, including yogurt in the leavened dough. The toasted garlic gives it that flavor you find in restaurants, too. By molding it into the bottom wells of spherical ice cube trays, you can make these breads uniform and top them with the Zucchini-Lemon Raita (see page 129 for the recipe) for a lovely snack.

2 cloves garlic, minced

1 teaspoon olive oil

Freshly ground sea salt and black pepper to taste

¼ cup warm water

1 teaspoon sugar

1 teaspoon active dry yeast

1½ cups flour

¼ teaspoon salt

¼ cup milk

¼ cup plain yogurt

2 tablespoons melted butter

2 tablespoons minced parsley or cilantro

Lay out a pair of 6-well, 2-inch sphere ice cube trays. Spray or brush them with cooking oil.

Preheat the oven to 350°F.

On a small sheet pan, mix the garlic with the olive oil, salt, and pepper. Spread out the mixture in a single layer. Place it into the oven and toast until it is aromatic and golden brown. Take care not to burn. Set aside. Do not turn off the oven.

In a bowl, mix the water with the sugar and yeast. Allow to foam, about 10 minutes.

In another bowl, mix the flour with the salt.

Oil a third bowl. Set aside.

Add the milk and yogurt to the foamy water and whisk until combined. Add the liquids to the flour and salt and mix until a dough forms.

Turn out the dough onto a floured surface and punch it down. Knead again very briefly and divide in half. (If you like your flatbread very thin, divide the dough into thirds for three batches.) Form ½ of the dough into a thin tube. With a sharp knife, cut into 12 equal pieces, then shape each piece into a ball. Roll out or with a palm press each piece so that it is roughly the

(continued on next page)

size and shape of the ice cube tray well. Place each one in an ice cube tray well. Repeat the process with the second half of the dough and have them ready to bake when the first batch comes out of the oven.

Bake for 10 to 15 minutes or until the bread is golden and puffy, with bubbles forming. Remove from the oven and brush with butter, then sprinkle with toasted garlic and parsley or cilantro. Bake the second batch, repeating the process. Unmold with tongs or a serving utensil.

Serve immediately as is or with a topping of your choice (see below).

THINK OUTSIDE THE TRAY

If you think of naan as the base, you can create a stunning array of little snacks. Top with sauce, cheese, and pepperoni and you have pizza naan. Sauté onions and peppers with an egg and you have breakfast naan. Cut up some salami, provolone cheese, and olives, and you have antipasto naan. Along those lines, try feta, cucumbers, and red onions for Greek salad naan, or tuna, hard-boiled egg, haricots verts, and boiled potatoes for salade Niçoise naan.

Tamago Crab Frittata

Ice Cube Tray: Honeycomb 🎩 Makes 37 cubes

Why go to a sushi bar when you can whip up these miniature crab-filled frittatas at home? The addition of mirin, dashi, and sugar give these little bites the flavor of Japan, but the texture is borrowed from Italy. Enjoy the fusion!

4 large eggs, beaten

¼ cup dashi stock
(or seafood or fish stock)

1 teaspoon mirin (or sweet white wine like Moscato)

½ teaspoon soy sauce

1 tablespoon sugar

⅓ cup minced lump crabmeat, picked over

Lay out a 37-well, honeycomb ice cube tray.

Preheat oven to 350°F.

In a bowl, mix the beaten eggs, dashi, mirin, soy sauce, and sugar until the sugar dissolves.

Mix in the crabmeat. Pour into the wells of the ice cube tray, evening out the liquid with a spoon or the whisk.

Place in oven and bake until the tops rise and turn golden, about 25 to 30 minutes. Cool and flip over to unmold. Use a knife to gently separate the honeycomb pieces from each other. Serve with ponzu or soy sauce for a little extra flavor if desired.

THINK OUTSIDE THE TRAY

Use any cooked, flaked white fish instead of more expensive crab—this is a super way to reinvent leftovers. Or for some really luxurious flavor, substitute lobster for the crab.

Creamed Corn bread Muffins
with Confetti Peppers

Ice Cube Tray: 1-Inch Square 🎩 Makes 15 miniature muffins

Sure, there are a million ways to make cornbread. But this recipe isn't just tasty—it's quick and easy. These cute little square muffins add a bit of decorative flair to any meal.

1 cup cornmeal

½ teaspoon salt

½ teaspoon baking soda

1 teaspoon baking powder

1 tablespoon sugar

½ cup creamed corn

½ cup milk

1 egg

½ cup red, yellow and green bell peppers, julienne, fingertip-size

Lay out a 15-well, 1-inch square ice cube tray.

Preheat the oven to 350°F.

In a bowl, combine the cornmeal, salt, baking soda, baking powder, and sugar.

In another bowl, mix together well the creamed corn, milk, egg, and peppers. Add the wet mixture to the dry ingredients and stir to create a pourable batter. If batter is too dry, add equal amounts of creamed corn and milk to moisten.

Divide the batter evenly between the wells of the ice cube tray.

Bake for 25 to 30 minutes or until the tops are golden brown and beginning to crack. Remove from oven and cool completely. Unmold and serve in a basket.

THINK OUTSIDE THE TRAY

If you like spice, use chili peppers instead of bell peppers. For added Asian flair, prepare the recipe for Mustard-Soy Glazed Shishito Peppers (see page 113) and add them to the cornbread batter.

Country Terrine

Ice Cube Tray: 2-Inch Square Makes 12 terrines

Making country-style pâté, or terrine, can seem very complicated. Indeed, if you read a chef's recipe for it, you might give up before you even start. But the truth is, it's no more complicated than a meatloaf. The method in which you cook it—in a bain-marie—not the ingredients changes the texture of the meats in it. These baby terrines are even easier to make, because the ice cube tray is practically designed to sit in a water bath.

2 tablespoons olive oil

1 small onion, chopped

1 clove garlic, minced

2 tablespoons Sauternes (or any brandy or Cognac)

½ pound (8 ounces) ground pork

¼ pound (4 ounces) ground veal

2 ounces calf liver or 2 chicken livers, ground

1 egg, beaten

1 teaspoon Dijon mustard

15 unsalted pistachios, shelled

¼ cup bread crumbs

1 teaspoon minced fresh thyme

1 teaspoon minced fresh sage

1 teaspoon minced fresh parsley

½ teaspoon ground cloves

½ teaspoon ground ginger

½ teaspoon nutmeg

Freshly ground sea salt and black pepper to taste

12 slices of raw bacon, cut in half

Lay out a pair of 6-well, 2-inch square ice cube trays.

Preheat oven to 350°F.

In a small pan, heat olive oil over medium heat. Add onion and stir. When onion begins to sweat, add garlic. When the onion is translucent, about 5 minutes cooking time total, remove the mixture from the heat. Stir in the Sauternes and allow to sit.

In a bowl, place all the remaining ingredients except the bacon. Add the onion mixture and combine well by hand.

Shape some meat, about the size and shape of a well, in the palm of your hand. Wrap it in a half piece of bacon to cover two sides. Turn and wrap another piece of bacon around the parts that are uncovered. It should now look like a square of meat wrapped in bacon. Squeeze lightly to make sure there are no air pockets between the meat and the bacon. Deposit it in a well; it should fit perfectly. Repeat until all wells are filled. Cover the entire tray with parchment paper, then foil.

Stand the ice cube tray in another baking or casserole dish. Fill the larger dish with water until it comes halfway up the ice cube tray.

(continued on next page)

Place in oven and bake for 45 minutes, then pierce a terrine to test. If the juice runs clear, the terrine is done. If it runs pink, cook for another 5 minutes. Repeat until terrine is finished.

Remove from the oven. While terrines are cooling, weight them so that they reabsorb their juices. Chill overnight before serving.

There may be extra congealed fat when you unmold. This flecks away easily when it's cold, so do it immediately when you remove the terrines from the trays. You can keep or unwrap from the bacon. Serve each terrine sliced with French bread or crackers and cornichons and/or cocktail onions, along with olives.

THINK OUTSIDE THE TRAY

Don't feel obligated to use organ meats if they don't appeal to you. Substitute any of the ground red meats for chicken or turkey. Replace the pistachios with macadamia nuts. Add more herbs, or use kale (if you must!) and spinach to green it up. There are no limits on how to make terrine.

CORNICHONS AND COCKTAIL ONIONS

Cornichons are tiny French pickles cured in vinegar and tarragon. They have a very specific flavor and texture, and in my opinion, are absolutely necessary on a charcuterie plate of any kind. If you can't find cornichons—they're usually available in specialty markets—you can substitute baby kosher dills. Although they don't have quite the same texture or flavor because a) they're not the same kind of cucumber, and b) they're pickled with different spices, they will provide the necessary bite to cut the richness of the terrine.

Cocktail onions are pearl onions pickled in a lightly flavored brine. In this case, the natural flavor of the onion makes them a touch sweeter, but the requisite crunch is there to counteract the soft texture of the terrine. So they also serve as an excellent counterpoint.

Quick Cracker Crumb Quiche

Ice Cube Tray: 1-Inch Square 🧊 Makes 30 miniature quiches

I could eat miniature quiches all day long. They never seem to fill me up. That's why I tend to whip up a large batch. This recipe could be halved or doubled, depending on how much you like quiche, or how many you want to serve.

2 cups Ritz cracker crumbs

8 tablespoons melted butter

8 eggs, beaten

½ cup half-and-half

1½ cups shredded Swiss or cheddar cheese, divided

½ cup cooked and drained spinach, chopped

4 tablespoons chopped scallions

Freshly ground sea salt and black pepper to taste

Lay out a pair of 15-well, 1-inch square ice cube trays.

Preheat the oven to 350°F.

In a bowl, mix Ritz crumbs and butter together. Divide evenly—about a generous ½ teaspoon for each—and press into the bottoms of the ice cube tray wells.

In another bowl, combine the eggs, half-and-half, 1 cup of cheese, spinach, scallions, and salt and pepper together.

Dividing evenly, fill the wells a little bit short of the tops. Scatter the remaining half of the shredded cheese on top of the wells.

Bake for 25 to 30 minutes or until the egg is set throughout and the tops are golden brown. Unmold carefully while warm and serve as finger food.

THINK OUTSIDE THE TRAY

You can flavor these quiches with any vegetables or meats that you like. Broccoli, onions and peppers, ham—it all works. Just remember to keep the dice very small and in proportion with the quiche itself, or you'll wind up with a big chunk of ham and no egg in the well of the ice cube tray.

Horseradish-Bacon Cheddar Cheese Balls

Ice Cube Tray: Mini Sphere 🔵 Makes 36 cheese balls

One thing I love about making your own horseradish-bacon-cheddar mix—you get to control the ratio of heat and salty goodness. In other words, mix in as much horseradish and bacon as you like. This recipe treads middle ground, so feel free to ramp it up according to your preference.

¾ cup cheddar cheese spread, room temperature

1 tablespoon horseradish

2 pieces cooked bacon, minced

Lay out a 36-well, mini sphere ice cube tray.

In a bowl or in a food processor, blend the cheese, horseradish, and bacon together. Dividing evenly, fill the wells of the trays and refrigerate for at least 4 hours before unmolding. You can also freeze these cheese balls for a firmer texture and prettier appearance. Unmold by popping them out and serve them on a plate with crackers. Or, if frozen, pour them in a bowl and offer toothpicks.

THINK OUTSIDE THE TRAY

If you enjoy a salty-sweet partnership, replace the horseradish with a tablespoon of maple syrup. Or if you really like pungency, add a tablespoon of mustard; one with seeds will also supply more texture.

French Onion Cheese Balls

Ice Cube Tray: Mini Sphere 🍶 Makes 36 cheese balls

Sure, you can buy flavored cheeses. But it's so much more impressive to make your own. These bite-sized delicacies don't last long on any cheese tray, though, so it might be a good idea to make a double batch.

1 tablespoon flour

½ teaspoon dried thyme

Freshly ground salt and pepper to taste

½ onion, diced

1 tablespoon butter

1 tablespoon olive oil

1 tablespoon dry sherry

8 ounces (1 package) cream cheese, room temperature

4 ounces (1 small log) creamy goat cheese, room temperature

Lay out a 36-well, mini sphere ice cube tray.

In a bowl, mix the flour with the dried thyme, salt, and pepper. Add the diced onions and mix until the onion pieces are lightly dusted.

In a sauté pan, melt the butter and olive oil together over low heat. Add the floured onions and cook, stirring, until the onions are caramelized, about 20 minutes. Add the sherry and cook for another 5 minutes. Remove from the heat and allow to cool completely.

In another bowl or in a food processor, blend the cream cheese and goat cheese together. Add the onions and mix well. Dividing evenly, fill the wells of the trays and refrigerate for at least 4 hours before unmolding. You can also freeze these cheese balls for a firmer texture and prettier appearance. Unmold by popping them out and serve them on a plate with crackers. Or, if frozen, pour them in a bowl and offer toothpicks.

THINK OUTSIDE THE TRAY

Any soft, white, spreadable cheese will be an asset in this recipe. Replace the goat cheese with mascarpone, ricotta, Boursin, or even a double or triple crème cheese to add flavor to the cream cheese.

Mini Mains

Mama's Veal Meatloaf with Tomato-Oregano Sauce   75

Southern Shrimp and Grits   76

Pear and Ricotta Mini Herbed Ravioli with Manchego Alfredo Sauce   77

Carbonara Polenta Squares   79

Rotisserie Chicken Pot Pie   80

Taco Salad Cups with Smoky Enchilada Sauce and Key Lime Sour Cream   82

Tuna Poke Balls   84

Open-Face Egg Rolls with Stir-Fry and Thai-Style Peanut Sauce   87

Barbecue Sliced Steak Steamed Biscuits with Hoisin Gastrique
and Vinegar Cucumbers   89

Ground Beef Empanadas   93

Stuffed Cabbage with Golden Raisin Sweet-n-Sour Sauce   95

Mozzarella-Stuffed Meatballs with Sundried Tomato Sauce   98

THINK OUTSIDE THE TRAY

Freeze the Tomato-Oregano
Sauce in a heart ice cube tray
to show how Mama really feels
about her meatloaf. The hearts
will melt—literally—onto the
baked meat and add just the
right amount of flavor.

Mama's Veal Meatloaf
with Tomato-Oregano Sauce

Ice Cube Tray: 2-Inch Square 🎩 Makes 6 squares

½ pound ground veal

1 clove garlic, minced

½ onion, finely chopped

1 carrot, finely chopped

½ yellow or orange bell pepper, finely chopped

¼ cup seasoned bread crumbs

1 egg

2 tablespoons ketchup

2 tablespoons minced fresh parsley

Freshly ground sea salt and black pepper to taste

½–1 cup Tomato-Oregano Sauce (see recipe below)

Lay out a 6-well, 2-inch square ice cube tray.

Preheat oven to 350°F.

In a bowl, combine all the ingredients except for the Tomato-Oregano Sauce. Mix with your hands or a spatula until just combined. Do not overwork the meat.

Dividing evenly, fill the wells. Place in the oven and bake until the top is crusty and beginning to brown, about 25 to 30 minutes. Allow to rest for 5 to 10 minutes after removing from the oven to reabsorb the juices. Unmold with a mini spatula and plate with the Tomato-Oregano Sauce on top.

Tomato-Oregano Sauce
Makes about 1 cup

2 tablespoons olive oil

1 clove garlic, minced

½ onion, chopped

1 (8-ounce) can plain tomato sauce, smooth or chunky

2 tablespoons minced fresh oregano

Freshly ground sea salt and black pepper to taste

In a sauté pan, heat olive oil over a low flame. Add garlic and onions and stir until translucent.

Add tomato sauce and cook at a simmer for 15 minutes. Add oregano and season with salt and pepper to taste. Cook for another 5 minutes.

Southern Shrimp and Grits

Ice Cube Tray: 2-Inch Square 🍧 Makes 12 cubes

The corn flavor in this grits recipe is somewhat subdued, thanks to stock and milk. The smoky cheese and butter also tend to obscure the grits a bit. If you want to heighten the flavor instead, eliminate both the stock and the milk and use only water.

2 cups stock, any flavor (can substitute water)

2 cups milk (can substitute water)

1 cup stone-ground grits

2 tablespoons butter

1 tablespoon minced parsley

1 cup corn

1 cup smoked, shredded Gouda or cheddar

Freshly ground sea salt and black pepper to taste

2 tablespoons olive oil

½ onion, chopped

½ bell pepper, chopped

1 tablespoon smoked paprika

1 tablespoon fresh lemon juice

12 large shrimp, peeled and deveined

¼ cup tomato sauce

1 tablespoon fresh thyme

Lay out a pair of 6-well, 2-inch square ice cube trays. Spray or brush with them cooking oil.

Preheat the oven to 350°F.

In a pot, bring the broth and milk to a boil. Stir in the grits and butter. Allow to cook for 20 to 25 minutes or until the liquid is completely absorbed.

Remove from heat and mix in the parsley, corn, and cheese. Season with salt and pepper to taste.

Dividing evenly, fill the wells of the ice cube trays and place in the oven. Bake for 25 to 30 minutes until the cubes are firm to the touch and turning golden-brown on top.

Meanwhile, in a pan over medium heat, warm the olive oil. Add the onion and bell pepper and sauté until the onion is translucent. Add the paprika and lemon juice and stir to coat.

Add the shrimp and sear on both sides until they curl up and turn pink, about 4 minutes. Deglaze the pan with tomato sauce, add the thyme, and simmer until just hot, then remove from the heat. Set aside.

Remove the grits from the oven. Slide a dull knife blade around the edges of the squares to loosen them. Unmold carefully with a mini spatula. To plate, spoon a little sauce on the bottom, set a square of grits on top, then garnish with a shrimp. Serve immediately.

•∘•⦁∘•⦁∘⦁∘⦁∘•⦁∘∘•⦁∘∘•⦁∘⦁∘∘•⦁∘•⦁∘∘⦁∘•⦁∘•

THINK OUTSIDE THE TRAY

Grits are frequently flavored with bacon or sausage for extra zest. Sauté small chunks of andouille sausage and then add them to the grits before filling the tray.

Pear and Ricotta Mini Herbed Ravioli
with Manchego Alfredo Sauce

Ice Cube Tray: Rectangular Makes 24–36 rectangles

Ice cube trays serve as a guide to making ravioli. By draping the pasta dough over the wells, you take the guesswork out of measuring and create the exact same size ravioli every time. This recipe works best in the old-fashioned, harder plastic or metal trays, not the floppier silicone trays. But you can use either.

4 eggs, divided

3 tablespoons water, divided

¼ minced ripe pear

¾ cup ricotta cheese

Freshly ground sea salt and black pepper to taste

1½ cups all-purpose flour

½ tablespoon minced rosemary

½ tablespoon minced thyme

½ tablespoon minced oregano

¼ teaspoon salt

1–2 cups Manchego Alfredo Sauce (see recipe on page 78)

Lay out a 12-well, rectangular tray.

In a small bowl, beat an egg with a tablespoon of water. Set aside.

In another bowl, mix the pear with the ricotta, one egg, salt and pepper. Set aside.

In a food processor, combine the flour, 2 eggs, rosemary, thyme, oregano, and salt. Blend until a dough forms. If too crumbly, add 1 to 2 tablespoons of water.

Turn out the dough onto a lightly floured surface. Knead for 1 to 2 minutes until smooth. Form a ball and wrap it in plastic wrap. Allow to sit for 30 minutes.

Unwrap the dough and cut it into 4 sections. With a rolling pin or in a pasta machine, roll out one section until it is just larger than the width and length of the ice cube tray. Drape it over the tray and tuck it gently into the wells.

Brush the pasta with the reserved egg mixture. Place about a teaspoon of the pear mixture into each well.

(continued on next page)

Roll out another section of dough until it is just larger than the width and length of the tray. Brush it with the egg mixture. Place it egg-side down over the filled wells, matching the sheets as closely as possible. Roll a pin over the top of the second sheet of dough, sealing the ravioli. Turn the tray over and unmold the ravioli. You may need to crimp a bit by hand or separate by pizza cutter or knife as well.

Repeat the process until all the dough and filling has been used. (If you have extra dough leftover and it's not enough to make more ravioli, you can use the scraps to make orecchiette pasta with your thumb.)

To cook, boil a pot of salted water and simmer the ravioli until they float, about 2 to 3 minutes. You can also freeze them for future use. Top with Manchego Alfredo Sauce and serve in a shallow bowl immediately.

Manchego Alfredo Sauce

Makes 2–3 cups

2 tablespoons butter

2 tablespoons olive oil

1 clove garlic, minced

2 tablespoons flour

1 cup milk

½ cup heavy cream

Freshly ground sea salt and black pepper to taste

1 cup shredded Manchego cheese

½ cup grated Parmesan cheese

In a saucepan, melt the butter and olive oil over low heat. Add the garlic and sauté until fragrant. Whisk in the flour until no lumps are left. Add the milk and cream and season with salt and pepper to taste. Bring to a boil, then reduce to a simmer for about 2 to 3 minutes. The mixture should be thick enough to stick to the utensil.

Add the cheeses and stir until they are completely melted. Use immediately.

THINK OUTSIDE THE TRAY

Pear is a natural with cheeses of all kinds, but some people just don't like its flavor or consistency. That's okay. Any fruit—fig? apple? dates?—or even a vegetable will work here. Try something seasonal like pumpkin, cut down on the ricotta, and adjust the spices in the pasta to match. Once you master the technique, the filling is up to you.

Carbonara Polenta Squares

Ice Cube Tray: 1-Inch Square 🧊 Makes 30 polenta squares

Made with ingredients you usually have hanging around the fridge, this recipe is so addictive that it's difficult to share. I suggest making the full recipe of two trays—one for yourself, another for anyone else who happens to be around. It's also a plum game-day snack, especially if you serve the squares with the tangy Tomato-Oregano Sauce that accompanies the Mama's Veal Meatloaf (see page 75 for the recipe). But you can also cut this recipe in half easily if you're on your own for an evening or two.

2 cups chicken stock

1 cup dry polenta

2 tablespoons olive oil

1 clove minced garlic

4 ounces pancetta or guanciale, sliced into small strips or chunks

2 eggs

½ cup grated Parmesan

1 tablespoon minced Italian parsley

Freshly ground sea salt and black pepper to taste

THINK OUTSIDE THE TRAY

Classic carbonara has no vegetables in it, but that's no reason why you can't include any. Peas would add a nice pop, and carrots some color as well as flavor. If you don't want to bake the vegetables with the polenta, think about cutting the rich flavor with some faintly bitter greens like sautéed arugula or broccoli rabe that you can serve on the side.

Lay out a pair of 15-well, 1-inch square ice cube trays. Spray or brush them with cooking oil.

Preheat the oven to 350°F.

In a pot, boil the chicken stock. Add the polenta. Stir continuously while it cooks for the next 20 to 30 minutes.

Meanwhile, in a skillet, heat the olive oil. Add the garlic and pancetta or guanciale and sauté until the meat is crisp. Remove the meat with a slotted spoon. Set aside. Reserve the fat and set aside.

In a bowl, beat the eggs. Add the Parmesan, parsley, and salt and pepper and whisk together.

When the polenta is cooked, remove from the heat and stir in 1 to 2 tablespoons of the reserved fat. Quickly whisk in the pancetta or guanciale and the egg mixture.

Dividing evenly, fill the wells, and place in the oven. Bake for 20 to 25 minutes or until the edges are crisp. Slide a dull knife blade around the edges of the squares to loosen them. Unmold carefully with a mini spatula. Serve on a platter to pass as appetizers or plate with greens as a light meal.

Rotisserie Chicken Pot Pie

Ice Cube Tray: 2-Inch Square ⬯ Makes 12 pot pies

This is one of the few recipes in the book that uses store-bought, ready-made ingredients. It's for those nights when you've had a long day and want to get something in the oven fast, but you're tired of the same-old rotisserie chicken dinner. With just a few ingredients to negotiate, this dish is ready in minutes—as long as you remember to put the pastry in the refrigerator the night before to thaw out, that is.

12 frozen puff pastry shells, thawed

2 tablespoons butter

1 tablespoon flour

1 cup chicken stock

½ cup milk

Freshly ground sea salt and black pepper to taste

1 cup chopped rotisserie chicken

½ cup frozen peas and carrots mix

¼ cup frozen pearl onions

Lay out a pair of 6-well, 2-inch square ice cube trays.

Preheat the oven to 350°F.

Tear the top ring portion of the pastry rounds from the main circles and reserve. Manipulate and stretch the main circles into squares. Maneuver them into the ice cube wells so that they cover the bottom and then stretch up the sides. You can use a little of the reserved rings to reinforce the bottoms if necessary.

In a saucepan, melt the butter over low heat. Whisk in the flour until no lumps are left, then add the chicken stock ½ cup at a time. Add the milk and season with salt and pepper to taste. Bring to a boil, then reduce to a simmer. The mixture should be thick enough to stick to the utensil.

Add the chicken, peas and carrots, and pearl onions. Mix until all is incorporated. Remove from the heat and spoon the mixture evenly into the shells.

Use the reserved rings to make a crosshatch of pastry on top of each well.

Place in the oven and bake until the pastry is golden brown, about 25 minutes. Unmold carefully with a mini spatula and plate two per person.

THINK OUTSIDE THE TRAY

Change it to beef pot pie by switching the chicken for leftover steak, and substituting beef stock for chicken stock. Lamb also works really well in these open-face structures, as does turkey.

Taco Salad Cups
with Smoky Enchilada Sauce
and Key Lime Sour Cream

Ice Cube Tray: 2-Inch Sphere 🧊 Makes 9 taco cups

These little cups have a few different moving parts, and require some assembly. But then! If you can bear the cuteness overload, you're off to a fun and fabulous Taco Tuesday (or Thursday, or whatever day of the week you choose). If you want to really chow down, though, you might have to make a couple of trays.

3 small corn tortillas

Canola or vegetable oil cooking spray

¼ head iceberg lettuce, shredded

½ red onion, finely diced

2 vine-ripe tomatoes, chopped

1 (2.25-ounce) can sliced black olives, drained

½ pound ground turkey, sautéed in Smoky Enchilada Sauce (see recipe on page 83)

½–1 cup shredded cheddar or jack cheese

½–1 cup Key Lime Sour Cream (see recipe on page 83)

2 tablespoons minced fresh cilantro

Lay out a 6-well, 2-inch sphere ice cube tray.

Preheat the oven to 350°F.

Heat the stack of corn tortillas until warm by wrapping them in damp paper towels and putting them in the microwave for 15 seconds.

Remove one tortilla from the pile. Coat it on one side with cooking spray and, using a very sharp knife, cut it into four. Nestle two quarters together, spray-side down, into a well to form a bowl. Spray the interior of the bowl once it's formed. Repeat with the remaining tortillas.

Bake for 15 to 20 minutes or until tortilla bowls are crisp and begin to brown. Remove from the oven. Allow to cool slightly, then carefully remove the bowls from the trays. Place on a serving platter to fill.

Dividing evenly, lay the lettuce in the bottom of each cup. Repeat with the onions, tomatoes, and black olives. Top with the ground turkey sautéed in Smoky Enchilada Sauce and shredded cheese. Garnish with a tablespoon of Key Lime Sour Cream and minced cilantro.

Serve immediately. No plates are necessary—but plenty of napkins are!

Smoky Enchilada Sauce

Makes 2 cups

2 tablespoons vegetable oil

1 small onion, chopped

1 tablespoon chili powder

1 tablespoon smoked paprika

1 teaspoon cumin

1 teaspoon cayenne pepper (optional)

1 (15-ounce) can tomato sauce

Freshly ground sea salt and black pepper to taste

In a saucepan over medium heat, warm the oil. Add the onion and sauté until translucent. Add the spices and stir well.

When the onions are coated with the spices, pour in the tomato sauce. Salt and pepper to taste. Bring to a boil, then reduce to a simmer and cook for 15 minutes.

Key Lime Sour Cream

Makes 1 cup

1 cup sour cream, drained

Juice of 1 key lime

½ teaspoon cayenne pepper

Freshly ground sea salt and black pepper to taste

In a bowl, mix all the ingredients together. Keep in the refrigerator if not using immediately. Chill any remaining sour cream for up to 1 week.

THINK OUTSIDE THE TRAY

For extra garnishing fun, freeze the Key Lime Sour Cream in a thematic Decorative Ice Cube Tray, like stars or cacti, until just frozen enough to hold together for service. It takes about 1 to 2 hours. (Sour cream doesn't keep well in the freezer, so do this only on the day you're making the tacos.) You can do the same with the Smoky Enchilada Sauce, but you'll have to make a double batch, since you'll be using the sauce to cook the ground turkey.

HOW TO THICKEN SOUR CREAM NATURALLY

To drain sour cream and make it thicker, line a fine mesh colander with a coffee filter, then add the sour cream. The coffee filter will keep the thicker cream from running through the filter but allow the thinner liquid to escape. You can also use paper towels. This method works with yogurt as well and is helpful to take the water out of any minced vegetables such as cucumbers.

Tuna Poke Balls

Ice Cube Tray: 2-Inch Sphere ⬡ Makes 6 poke balls

This recipe takes the poke bowl trend and puts it in your hand by wrapping it in sushi rice. My son suggested this one—he's a huge fan of poke, sushi, tartare, ceviche, and all other kinds of raw to lightly cooked fish—and when I tried it, I could see instantly that it was a keeper.

2–2½ cups Sushi Rice (see recipe on page 85)

2 teaspoons soy sauce

¼ teaspoon sesame oil

¼ teaspoon prepared wasabi

4 ounces sushi-grade tuna, diced

¼ cup chopped English cucumber, seeded

¼ cup toasted white sesame seeds

Lay out a 6-well, 2-inch sphere ice cube tray.

Prepare Sushi Rice. Set aside to cool. When cool, divide into 6 portions.

In a bowl, whisk the soy sauce, sesame oil, and wasabi together until the wasabi has dissolved. Add the tuna and cucumber and mix until combined.

Pour the sesame seeds on a plate.

In the palm of your hand, mold half of one portion of rice into a half-circle. Leaving the sauce in the bowl, add ⅙ of the tuna-cucumber mixture in the center. Using the second half of the single portion of rice, close the rice into a ball the same size and shape as the ice cube tray well.

Roll the rice ball lightly in the sesame seeds and place in the well. Repeat the process for the rest of the remaining portions.

Once all the wells are filled, place the cover on the ice cube tray and allow to rest for 15 minutes.

Unmold with your fingers—these should pop right out—and serve on plates with side dishes of soy sauce and wasabi if desired.

Sushi Rice

Makes 3 cups

1 cup sushi rice (short-grained, glutinous, or sticky rice)

2 cups water

2 tablespoons rice vinegar

2 tablespoons sugar

½ teaspoon salt

Place the rice in a strainer and rinse it until the water runs clear.

In a saucepan, bring the water to a boil. Add the rice and cook until the water is absorbed and the rice is tender, about 20 minutes. Allow the rice to cool.

Meanwhile, in another pot, heat the vinegar over a low flame and add the sugar and salt. Simmer until the sugar and salt are dissolved.

Add the vinegar mixture to the rice and fold gently in a paddling motion; do not break the rice grains. The rice grains will become sticky as they dry.

THINK OUTSIDE THE TRAY

If you have a fishmonger you trust and love sushi or sashimi, you can use this recipe with any fresh, raw fish, from salmon to yellowtail to mackerel. If you don't, try cooked shrimp—you can even batter it with tempura coating first and fry it for extra crunch—and pair it with asparagus. I like to layer thinly sliced avocado on top when I serve this for a little bit of creamy mouthfeel, but you can also simply replace the tuna with avocado and make this a vegan dish.

Open-Face Egg Rolls
with Stir-Fry and Thai-Style Peanut Sauce

Ice Cube Tray: 2-Inch Sphere 🎩 Makes 6 stir-fry cups

Jazz up your average, everyday stir-fry by serving it in an egg roll cup. The cups are a cinch to make, and because they're not deep-fried, don't add a lot of calories. They can also replace rice, so you're cutting down on carbs by using them to hold the vegetables.

2 round egg roll wrappers

Canola or vegetable oil cooking spray

1 teaspoon sugar

1 tablespoon cornstarch

½ cup water

2 tablespoons soy sauce

2 tablespoons peanut oil

½ sweet onion, sliced

½ yellow or orange bell pepper, sliced

½ head broccoli, roughly chopped

1 cup shredded cabbage

1 (8-ounce) can sliced water chestnuts, drained

1 teaspoon sesame oil

1 clove garlic, minced

1 teaspoon fresh minced ginger

½–1 cup Thai-Style Peanut Sauce (see recipe on page 88)

2 scallions, sliced on a bias

Lay out a 6-well, 2-inch sphere ice cube tray.

Preheat oven to 350°F.

Remove one wrapper from the pile. Coat it on one side with cooking spray. With a very sharp knife, cut it into quarters. Nestle two quarters together, sprayed side down, into a well to form a bowl. Spray the inside of the bowl once its formed. Repeat with the remaining wrappers.

Bake for 15 to 20 minutes or until egg roll bowls are crisp and begin to brown. Remove from the oven. Allow to cool slightly, then carefully remove the bowls from the trays. Place on dinner plates.

Meanwhile, in a small bowl, mix sugar, cornstarch, water, and soy sauce together. Set aside.

Heat a wok over a high flame and add the peanut oil. When the oil begins to smoke, quickly stir-fry the onion, pepper, broccoli, cabbage, and water chestnuts. After 2 to 3 minutes, push the vegetables to the edges and make a well in the middle. Add the sesame oil, garlic, and ginger. Stir for 1 minute, then add the water-soy sauce mixture and stir for 1 more minute. Reincorporate the vegetables to coat with the sauce and remove from the wok.

(continued on next page)

Divide the vegetables evenly among the egg roll bowls and top with Thai-Style Peanut Sauce. Garnish with scallions.

Serve immediately with any extra stir-fried vegetables on the side.

Thai-Style Peanut Sauce

Makes 1½ cups

1 cup peanut butter

2 tablespoons peanut oil

2 tablespoons soy sauce

1 tablespoon fresh lime juice

1 teaspoon light brown sugar

2 tablespoons coconut milk (can substitute water)

1 teaspoon minced fresh ginger

1 clove garlic, minced

½ teaspoon red pepper flakes

In a bowl or food processor, mix all ingredients together until well blended. If the sauce is too thick for your taste, thin with water. If too thin, add more peanut butter.

THINK OUTSIDE THE TRAY

Peanut butter and peanut products freeze extremely well. There's nothing stopping you from piping the Thai-Style Peanut Sauce into a decorative ice cube tray—stars, hearts, or flowers—and creating garnishes for your stir-fry egg roll bowls. This helps with preparation time, too, because you can make the sauce anytime and keep it in the freezer, then just quickly whip up the stir-fry.

Barbecue Sliced Steak Steamed Biscuits
with Hoisin Gastrique and Vinegar Cucumbers

Ice Cube Tray: 2-Inch Sphere 🎩 Makes 12 biscuits

Bao buns, from which I took this recipe's inspiration, are usually prepared in a steamer. Interestingly, a spherical ice cube tray, which has a cover with a tiny little hole in the top of each well, acts in a similar manner. Just make sure to place the cover on top of the ice cube tray before you bake these puffy little pieces of heaven, or you won't achieve the correct consistency. The difference between these and actual bao buns, of course, lies in the shape. Bao buns are folded; these are tucked into the wells to give them a bell-like shape.

½ cup hot water

1 teaspoon yeast

1 tablespoon sugar

½ tablespoon vegetable oil

1½ cups flour

1 teaspoon sesame oil

½ cup Hoisin Gastrique
(see recipe on page 91)

Barbecue Sliced Steak
(see recipe on page 91)

Vinegar Cucumbers
(see recipe on page 92)

6 sprigs cilantro

1–2 handfuls fresh bean sprouts

Lay out a pair of 6-well, 2-inch sphere ice cube trays. Spray or brush the bottoms with cooking oil.

Preheat the oven to 350°F.

In a bowl, dissolve the yeast and sugar in the hot water. The mixture should foam a little. Add the oil and the flour, then work into a dough.

Turn out onto a lightly floured surface and knead for about 5 minutes or until the dough is smooth and elastic. Place in a lightly oiled bowl, cover with a damp kitchen towel, and allow to rise in a warm place for about 45 minutes or until the dough has doubled in size.

Turn out the dough on parchment paper and punch it down. Shape it into a log about 1½ inches in diameter and cut it into 12 pieces. Roll each piece into a ball, then flatten with your hand or, with a rolling pin, roll them out until they are the size and shape of the ice cube tray bottoms. Brush the tops with sesame oil. Cover with another towel. Allow to rise for 15 minutes.

(continued on next page)

Mold each biscuit into the bottom of an ice cube tray well. Cover the ice cube tray with the top and place in the oven. Bake for 20 to 25 minutes or until the buns are steamed through.

Add a little Hoisin Gastrique in the bottom of each biscuit, then line with two pieces of Barbecue Sliced Steak, a couple of Vinegar Cucumbers, a sprig of cilantro, and a few bean sprouts. Serve immediately. You can eat these as handheld items, but they get a little messy. Plates will catch the fallout.

Barbecue Sliced Steak

½ cup ketchup

2 tablespoons soy sauce

1 teaspoon sesame oil

1 tablespoon fresh yuzu juice (or a mixture of lime and grapefruit juices)

1 teaspoon five-spice powder

1 clove garlic, minced

1 thumbnail-sized piece ginger, minced

Freshly ground sea salt and black pepper to taste

1 (12-ounce) boneless sirloin

In a bowl, combine all the ingredients except for the steak. Mix well.

Using a fork, poke the steak with holes to tenderize. Add the steak to the marinade and allow to sit for 3 to 4 hours or overnight in the refrigerator.

Remove from the marinade and bring to room temperature. Grill or pan-fry on one side for 4 minutes, then turn over and cook for another 4 minutes for medium rare. Remove from the heat and allow to rest for 5 minutes.

Slice into 12 portions to serve.

Note: You may have extra steak depending on the size and puffiness of your buns. Feel free to eat the beef without a bun!

Hoisin Gastrique

Makes about ½–¾ cup

¼ cup sugar

1 tablespoon water

1 garlic clove, minced

1 thumbnail-sized piece ginger, minced

2 tablespoons seasoned rice vinegar

¼ cup yuzu juice (or a mixture of lime and grapefruit juices)

¼ cup hoisin sauce

In a saucepan, cook sugar and water together without stirring over a low flame until the sugar caramelizes into a light golden color. Swirl the pan to move the sugar around and keep it from burning.

Add the garlic and ginger and stir for a minute. Add vinegar and yuzu juice and stir until the sugar is dissolved and the mixture turns syrupy.

Stir in hoisin sauce and turn up the flame to medium. Boil for 3 minutes and then remove from heat. The mixture should be thick enough to coat a spoon.

(continued on next page)

Vinegar Cucumbers

Makes about 2 cups

1 English cucumber, thinly sliced

1 cup seasoned rice vinegar

⅓ cup sugar

Freshly ground sea salt to taste

In a bowl, combine all the ingredients. Allow to marinate 3 to 4 hours before serving.

THINK OUTSIDE THE TRAY

Bao buns, which come from the word *baoizi* and are originally from China, can be filled with just about anything you desire. Likewise, these steamed biscuits can be stuffed with different stir-fry combinations. Or experiment with Korean, Thai, Indian, or Vietnamese flavors. They're awesome with kimchi and pork, tandoori chicken, or lemongrass-scented shrimp. For an extra-special touch, freeze the Hoisin Gastrique in a decorative ice cube tray and top the biscuits with the cubes for a garnish.

Ground Beef Empanadas

Ice Cube Tray: 2-Inch Sphere 🧊 Makes 24 empanadas

There are as many ways to make empanadas as there are Latin countries. Maybe, in fact, there are more ways to make empanadas. Living in Miami, I've eaten my fair share of these addictive, hand-held pies, stuffed with all manner of savory ingredients. Below is perhaps the most basic recipe, adapted to the spherical ice cube tray. See the Think Outside the Tray box for more ideas!

1 tablespoon olive oil

1 small onion, chopped

¼ pound ground beef

Freshly ground sea salt and black pepper to taste

1½ cups flour

¼ teaspoon salt

6 tablespoons cold unsalted butter

2 eggs, divided

¼ cup milk

1 hard-boiled egg, shelled and chopped

¼ cup cooked peas

6 green pitted olives, sliced

1 teaspoon chili powder

1 teaspoon garlic powder

Lay out a pair of 6-well, 2-inch sphere ice cube tray. Spray or brush them with cooking oil.

Preheat the oven to 350°F.

In a pan, heat the oil over a medium-low flame. Add the onion and sauté until translucent. Add the ground beef and season with salt and pepper. Cook, stirring, until the meat has browned thoroughly. Remove from heat, drain, and set aside.

In a food processor, combine the flour, salt, and butter. Pulse until the dough is crumbly. Add 1 egg and milk. Pulse again until a slightly smoother (but not sticky) dough forms. If dough is too sticky, add a little more flour.

Turn out the dough onto a lightly floured surface or piece of parchment paper and divide into two balls. Roll one ball into a tube and, with a sharp knife, cut it into 12 even pieces, then roll and flatten each piece into roughly the size and shape of the ice cube tray wells. Repeat the process with the other ball of dough. Allow the 24 flattened disks to rest.

In a bowl, combine the ground beef, hard-boiled egg, peas, and olives. Season with the chili powder,

(continued on next page)

garlic powder, and salt and pepper. Place a tablespoon of the mixture in the center of each disk. Do not use too much or they will be difficult to seal.

Bring the edges together to make a half-moon shape. To crimp, use a fork or your fingers to curl the edges. You might need to wet your fingers a bit to make them stick together if the dough has sat too long. It's also helpful, if using a fork, to crimp on both sides.

Beat the remaining egg. Brush one side of the sealed empanadas lightly with the egg, then place them brushed side down in the wells of the ice cube tray to bake 12 at a time. Brush the tops with the remaining egg. Place in the oven and bake for 15 minutes or until the empanadas are golden brown all over.

Remove from the oven. Using tongs or another serving utensil, transfer the cooked empanadas to a serving platter. Repeat the baking process with the remaining 12 empanadas. To serve, pass them as appetizers or plate several of them together with a vegetable and starch.

THINK OUTSIDE THE TRAY

Empanadas are a fantastic way to use up small amounts of leftover meats and vegetables. Try ham and cheese, minced chicken with vegetables, steak—whatever is hanging around in the refrigerator. Bind vegetables like corn or leafy greens with some cream and cheese and you're bound to please even the most stubborn, vegetable-resistant person in the family.

Stuffed Cabbage
with Golden Raisin Sweet-n-Sour Sauce

Ice Cube Tray: 2-Inch Sphere 🎩 Makes 8 cabbage rolls

This take on stuffed cabbage might even get the kids to try it, if only because it looks so adorable. The recipe makes 8 neat little packages, but as with all the Mini Mains, it's a snap to double or triple.

8 large, interior cabbage leaves

1 tablespoon vegetable oil

½ small onion, chopped

¼ cup golden raisins

½ pound ground beef

½ cup cooked white rice

1 egg

1 tablespoon ketchup

½ teaspoon cinnamon

1 teaspoon light brown sugar

Freshly ground sea salt and black pepper to taste

½–1 cup Golden Raisin Sweet-n-Sour Sauce (see recipe on page 97)

Lay out a pair of 4-well, 2-inch sphere ice cube trays.

Preheat oven to 350°F.

In the microwave or in a pot of boiling water, blanch the cabbage leaves until just soft and pliable, but not soggy. Remove from any liquid, dry on paper towels, and set aside.

In a sauté pan, heat the oil over a medium flame. Briefly sweat the onions for 2 minutes, then add the raisins, cooking until they plump, about 1 minute. Remove and allow to cool.

In a bowl, combine the ground beef with the onion-raisin mixture, rice, egg, ketchup, cinnamon, sugar, salt, and pepper. Divide into 1-ounce portions and roll into balls.

Place one ground beef ball in the center bottom of a cabbage leaf and wrap it in from the edges. Roll it until it is a tidy package with no ends sticking out. It should be the ideal size for an ice cube well. Repeat with the remaining seven balls and cabbage leaves.

Set one cabbage roll each inside an ice cube well. Cover the trays with their lids and place in the oven to bake for 15 minutes. When done, carefully unmold,

(continued on next page)

spear with toothpicks or tongs to lift out, and plate. Garnish with Golden Raisin Sweet-n-Sour Sauce and serve with egg noodles on the side.

Serve immediately.

Golden Raisin Sweet-n-Sour Sauce

Makes 1½ cups

½ cup water

1 tablespoon cornstarch

¼ cup cranberry juice

¼ cup ketchup

½ cup light brown sugar

½ cup apple cider vinegar

½ cup golden raisins

In a small bowl, mix together the water and cornstarch. Set aside.

In a saucepan over medium heat, add remaining ingredients together and stir until well blended. Cook for 5 minutes until simmering, then add cornstarch mixture. Cook for another 5 minutes to thicken. If the sauce is too thick and sweet for your taste, thin with vinegar. If too thin and tangy, add more ketchup and sugar.

THINK OUTSIDE THE TRAY

To make this a more colorful meal, try using different kinds of rice in the beef mixture and as a side dish. Brown, red, or black rice adds texture and hues to the plate. Or substitute different grains altogether, such as quinoa. For the sauce, prepare a double batch and freeze half of it in decorative ice cube trays such as pineapples or apples, then pop a few "cubes" on a scoop of fluffy rice just before serving.

Mozzarella-Stuffed Meatballs
with Sundried Tomato Sauce

Ice Cube Tray: 2-Inch Sphere 🎩 Makes 6 meatballs

Ice cube meatballs? I admit that when I first thought to make this, I thought it would fail. Instead, it was one of the recipes that came together immediately and without any complication. The trays are ideal molds for the ground beef and keep them in perfect form.

½ pound ground beef

1 clove garlic, minced

½ onion, finely chopped

¼ cup seasoned bread crumbs

¼ grated Parmesan cheese

1 egg

2 tablespoons minced fresh parsley

Freshly ground sea salt and black pepper to taste

6 thumb-sized nuggets of smoked mozzarella

½–1 cup Sundried Tomato Sauce (see recipe below)

Lay out a 6-well, 2-inch sphere ice cube tray.

Preheat oven to 350°F.

In a bowl, combine all the ingredients except for the smoked mozzarella and Sundried Tomato Sauce. Mix with your hands or a spatula until just combined. Do not overwork the meat.

Divide meat evenly into six piles. Roll one into a meatball. Insert a nugget of mozzarella into it. Close the meatball around it. Place in one of the wells. Repeat the process until all the wells are filled. Place the top on the tray—it should fit perfectly—and place in the oven. Bake for 30 minutes.

To unmold, lift off the top of the tray—be very careful about the steam—and remove the meatballs with tongs. Place on Italian bread with sauce or over pasta.

Sundried Tomato Sauce

Makes about 1½ cups

2 tablespoons olive oil

1 clove garlic, minced

½ onion, chopped

2 tablespoons chopped sundried tomatoes in oil, drained

1 (8-ounce) can plain tomato sauce, smooth or chunky

Freshly ground sea salt and black pepper to taste

½ cup cream

In a sauté pan, heat olive oil over a low flame. Add garlic and onions and stir until translucent.

Add sundried tomatoes and tomato sauce and cook at a simmer for 15 minutes. Season with salt and pepper to taste and remove from heat. When cooler, stir in cream.

THINK OUTSIDE THE TRAY

For lighter meatballs, use ground turkey or chicken. Or substitute ground veal for the beef. You can also try a mixture of meats. Serve over pasta for a hearty meal, or make a sub with a good, crusty roll.

Sides and Dressings

Shaved Asparagus Soufflé

Ice Cube Tray: 2-Inch Sphere 🧊 Makes 12 soufflés

It's easy to think of soufflés as dishes that are complicated and out of reach of the everyday cook. But that's not the case. In fact, they're fairly easy to put together, and when you factor in these already compartmentalized trays, it becomes even simpler. The trick here is oiling the ice cube tray well, so that the soufflés slide out easily without collapsing.

3 asparagus spears

2 tablespoons butter

2 tablespoons flour

1 cup hot milk

¼ teaspoon nutmeg

¼ teaspoon paprika

Freshly ground sea salt and white pepper to taste

4 egg yolks

5 egg whites

1 cup shredded Gruyère cheese

•••••••••••••••••••••••••••••••

THINK OUTSIDE THE TRAY

As long as you don't add large pieces that weigh down the mixture, you can substitute any vegetables for the asparagus. Stir a purée of spinach into the egg batter, or slivers of onions and peppers, or a tiny mince of broccoli.

Lay out a pair of 6-well, 2-inch sphere ice cube tray, bottoms only. Spray or brush them with cooking oil.

Preheat the oven to 375°F.

Parboil the asparagus. Dry and finely shave the heads and some of the stems. Discard the tougher portions.

In a saucepan, melt the butter over low heat. Whisk in the flour until no lumps are left. Let the butter-flour mixture foam.

Add the hot milk and season to taste. Bring to a boil, then reduce to a simmer for about 2 to 3 minutes. The mixture should be thick enough to stick to the utensil.

Remove from the heat and season with nutmeg, paprika, and salt and pepper. Whisk egg yolks in one by one.

Whip egg whites into stiff peaks. Alternating between the egg whites, Gruyère, and asparagus, mix them all in a quarter at a time.

Dividing evenly, fill the wells. Place in the oven and bake until the tops are puffy and golden brown, about 20 to 25 minutes. Allow to cool slightly. They will lose some of their air and deflate a little, but they will also be easier to remove. Unmold with a mini spatula. Then pass as appetizers or plate a few at a time with a green salad for a meal.

Mixed Mushroom Beggar's Purse

Ice Cube Tray: 2-Inch Square 🎩 Makes 6 beggar's purses

Frozen phyllo dough allows you to prepare these beginner's tarts quickly and easily. And if you forget to defrost the pastry in the refrigerator the night before, you can leave it on the countertop to thaw while you prepare the filling. It takes about 30 to 45 minutes to become warm and pliable.

1 roll phyllo dough, thawed

2 tablespoons butter

1 tablespoon flour

Freshly ground sea salt and black pepper to taste

½ onion, diced

1½ cups chopped mixed Portobello and white mushrooms

½ cup frozen baby peas

1 tablespoon minced fresh dill

THINK OUTSIDE THE TRAY

Any really fresh mushrooms will do. Try a mix of morels, cèpe, hen-of-the-woods, oyster mushrooms—whatever you can find in the market. The key to making a good mushroom tart really is in the quality of the mushroom.

Lay out a 6-well, 2-inch square ice cube tray.

Preheat the oven to 350°F.

Spray or brush a single phyllo sheet with oil, then fold it into thirds. Manipulate it into a well to cover the walls. Repeat with 5 more sheets.

In a saucepan, melt the butter over low heat. Whisk in the flour until no lumps are left, then season with salt and pepper.

Add the onion. Sauté until the onion is translucent.

Add the mushrooms and peas. Sauté until the mushrooms begin to release their juices.

Stir in the dill and remove from the heat. Spoon the mixture evenly into the shells.

Bring the corners of the dough together and twist.

Place in the oven and bake until the pastry is golden brown, about 25 minutes. Allow to cool slightly so that the dough doesn't rip when you remove them. Unmold by squeezing gently with tongs and lifting them out. Place on a platter and pass as appetizers or serve as a side dish with Mama's Veal Meatloaf (see page 75).

Baked Stuffed Baby Artichokes

Ice Cube Tray: 2-Inch Square 🧊 Makes 12 artichokes

12 baby artichokes, washed and trimmed (or jarred artichokes)

½ cup mayonnaise

½ cup grated Parmigiano-Reggiano

2 cloves minced garlic

2 tablespoons fresh parsley

2 tablespoons freshly squeezed lemon juice

1 cup bread crumbs

Freshly ground sea salt and black pepper to taste

12 cubes Maître d'Hôtel Butter (see page 123 for recipe)

Lay out a pair of 6-well, 2-inch square ice cube trays.

Preheat the oven to 350°F.

Prepare a pot of salted water large enough to cover the artichokes. On the stove, cover, heat, and bring to a boil. Add the artichokes and parboil for 5 minutes. (If using jarred artichokes, skip the parboiling.) Drain and place one artichoke upright in each ice cube tray well.

In a bowl, mix together the mayonnaise, Parmigiano-Reggiano, garlic, parsley, lemon juice, bread crumbs, and salt and pepper. Spread the leaves of each artichoke and stuff the mixture in between, dividing evenly. Place one piece of Maître d'Hôtel Butter on top of each artichoke.

Place in the oven and bake until artichokes are tender and golden brown, about 25 to 30 minutes. Unmold using tongs or another utensil to carefully lift artichokes out of the trays and place on plates.

THINK OUTSIDE THE TRAY

To make this dish vegan, eliminate the mayonnaise, cheese, and butter, and substitute corn or vegetable oil. For carnivores, crumble up some chorizo (or any flavorful sausage of your choice) in the mixture for additional texture.

Truffle Mac-n-Cheese Squares

Ice Cube Tray: 2-Inch Square 🧊 Makes 8 squares

Nobody doesn't love mac-n-cheese—especially when you include some kind of truffle flavoring. One thing that's awesome about making it in this kind of tray? No one gets more than their share. These squares permit you to dish it out, fair and square.

½ cup seasoned bread crumbs

¼ cup grated Parmesan

2 tablespoons butter

2 tablespoons flour

1 cup milk

Freshly ground sea salt and black pepper to taste

1½ cups shredded cheese

1 teaspoon truffle paste (or truffle oil)

2½ cups cooked cavatelli or another pasta

Lay out an 8-well, 2-inch square ice cube tray.

Preheat the oven to 350°F.

In a small bowl, combine the bread crumbs and Parmesan. Set aside.

In a saucepan, melt the butter over low heat. Whisk in the flour until no lumps are left. Add the milk and season with salt and pepper to taste. Bring to a boil, then reduce to a simmer for about 2 to 3 minutes. The mixture should be thick enough to stick to the utensil.

Add the cheese and truffle paste. Stir until the cheese is completely melted.

Fold in the pasta and stir to combine. Remove from the heat. Dividing evenly, spoon the mac-n-cheese into the wells. Sprinkle the breadcrumb mixture over the top and place the tray into the oven.

Place in the oven and bake until the top is golden brown, about 25 to 30 minutes. Slide a dull knife blade around the edges of the squares to loosen them. Unmold carefully with a mini spatula. Serve on plates with Rotisserie Chicken Pot Pie (page 80).

THINK OUTSIDE THE TRAY

Any cheese that easily melts can be folded into the sauce. I like making this with an assortment. Gruyère gives it a shaper edge, while smoked Gouda lends an irresistible aroma as well as flavor. I'm also partial to throwing in a little Gorgonzola every once in a while, which deepens the sauce. Not satisfied with only noodles and cheese? Peas and corn lend textural contrast, and bacon, shrimp, or chicken are natural add-ins.

Parmesan Breadsticks

Ice Cube Tray: Water Bottle 🍶 Makes 20 breadsticks

If you're like me, you've made breadsticks before—and they've come out all different shapes and sizes. The beauty of using these trays is that they're an ideal guide. This no-yeast, no-rise, and no-rolling-pin recipe is really just a simple pizza dough, which means you can adapt it to use with the 1-inch or 2-inch square trays to make deep-dish or Sicilian-style pizza. Just add Tomato-Organo Sauce (see page 75) and mozzarella cheese, and you're good to go.

¾ cup grated Parmesan

1 tablespoon garlic powder

1 teaspoon minced oregano

1 teaspoon red pepper flakes (optional)

Freshly ground sea salt and black pepper to taste

¾–1 cup water

1 tablespoon vegetable oil

2 cups flour

2 teaspoons baking powder

1 teaspoon salt

Lay out a pair of 10-well water bottle ice cube trays so that the top is inverted, fitting into the bottom rather than over it. (Substitute a trio of 4-well, water bottle ice cube trays that only have one part each.)

Preheat the oven to 350°F.

In a small bowl, mix the Parmesan, garlic powder, oregano, red pepper flakes, and salt and pepper together. Set aside.

In another bowl, mix the water and oil together. Set aside.

In a third bowl, mix the flour with the baking soda, salt, and ⅓ of the Parmesan mixture. Add the water to the flour mixture a little at a time, mixing with your hands, until a soft dough forms. If it's too sticky, add more flour; if it's too dry, add more water.

Scatter some flour on a dry surface. Strew ⅓ of the Parmesan mixture on top of the flour. Turn out the ball of dough onto that surface and knead it for 5 minutes.

Divide the dough in half. Stretch out the dough in a rectangle about the width of the ice cube trays until it's about 1 inch thick. Top the dough with remaining ⅓ of the Parmesan mixture, patting it into the dough.

(continued on next page)

Using a pizza cutter or a sharp knife dipped in water, cut the dough in 10 breadsticks. Place them into the well of a tray. Repeat with the remaining ball of dough.

Place the trays into the oven on the top rack and bake until lightly golden brown, about 25 to 30 minutes. Unmold using tongs. Serve with dipping sauce, or as a side to pasta.

THINK OUTSIDE THE TRAY

The breadsticks can take any seasoning or seeds. My favorite? An "everything bagel" mix of sesame, poppy, toasted onion, toasted garlic, and caraway. If you use seeds, make sure to moisten the breadsticks with either a little water or brush them with an egg wash first so that the seeds will stick. Pressing them in won't be enough.

Mustard-Soy Glazed Shishito Peppers

Ice Cube Tray: Water Bottle 🧊 Makes 24 peppers

Shishito peppers are slender, green, finger-like peppers with thin walls. An East Asian variety, the shishito is generally sweet, but once in a while a particularly bracing one grows. The "unknown" factor makes these peppers a fun challenge to eat. They're also particularly good sautéed, grilled, or roasted. They're frequently served in Asian restaurants as appetizers and side dishes.

24 shishito peppers, washed and dried

2 tablespoons Chinese mustard (or Dijon)

¼ cup soy sauce

1 teaspoon sesame oil

1 teaspoon peanut oil

1 teaspoon Chinese five-spice powder

Freshly ground sea salt and black pepper to taste

Lay out a trio of 4-well, water bottle ice cube trays.

Preheat the oven to 350°F.

Poke a tiny hole or two in each pepper with a fork or tip of a skewer. (The holes will allow the marinade to penetrate and keep the peppers from bursting when they're cooked.) Place all the peppers in a large bowl.

In another bowl, mix the mustard, soy, sesame oil, peanut oil, and Chinese five-spice powder together. Pour it over the peppers and toss them with tongs. Marinate for 15 minutes, tossing every 5 minutes.

Lay the peppers out in the trays, 2 peppers to each well. Bake for 15 minutes or until peppers are brown and beginning to blister.

Remove trays from the oven. Using tongs, place in a bowl, salt and pepper to taste, and serve while hot.

•‧‧•‧•‧‧•‧·‧·‧•‧•‧•‧·‧·‧•‧•‧•‧·‧·‧·‧•‧•‧•‧•‧•‧•‧·‧•‧•‧

THINK OUTSIDE THE TRAY

Try this preparation with any long, slim, fresh pepper that fits in the tray: banana, jalapeño, habanero. You can also use slices of peppers. Experiment with what's in the market! Eat them whole or add them to other recipes.

Candied Bacon Twists

Ice Cube Tray: Water Bottle 🎩 Makes 10–12 twists

If you love bacon, you'll fall head over heels for these crunchy-chewy sticks of goodness. It doesn't matter what kind of bacon you use—pork or turkey—as long as it's thick cut and relatively meaty. These twists look great, and taste even better, on top of avocado toast, eggs Benedict, or an omelet.

1 pound thick-cut bacon
(10–12 slices)

4 tablespoons molasses

2 tablespoons maple syrup

1 tablespoon apple cider vinegar

Juice of 1 lemon

Freshly ground black pepper to taste

Lay out a trio of 4-well, water bottle ice cube trays.

Preheat the oven to 350°F.

Lay out a baking sheet or wax paper. Separate the bacon slices and lay them out lengthwise.

In a bowl, combine the molasses, maple syrup, apple cider vinegar, lemon, and black pepper. Mix well.

With a pastry brush or the back of a spoon, swipe each piece of bacon with the molasses mixture. Turn over the bacon and repeat with the other side.

Hold a piece of bacon by its middle, allowing the sides to fall down. Twist the two sides together as tightly as possible. Fit into the water bottle ice cube slots. Repeat until all the slots are filled. Brush each twist one more time with sauce.

Place in the oven. Bake for 10 minutes. Remove from the oven. Using tongs or a fork, turn the twists over, being careful to maintain the shape, and baste lightly with sauce. Return to the oven and bake for another 10 minutes.

Remove the bacon from the oven, turn again, and baste with half of the remaining molasses mixture. Bake for 10 minutes.

(continued on next page)

Remove again, turn the twists over, and baste with the last half of the mixture. Return to the oven for a final time and bake another 10 minutes or until twists are crisp. For well-done bacon, bake an additional 5 minutes.

Remove from the oven. Unmold using tongs. Most of the grease should remain in the pan, but you may want to drain the bacon twists on a paper towel before serving.

THINK OUTSIDE THE TRAY

For a fruitier flavor, add minced dates or raisins to the molasses mixture. For a lighter flavor, replace molasses with honey. For a tangier flavor, replace maple syrup with ketchup or barbecue sauce. For heat, a dash or two of Tabasco sauce or your favorite chili peppers, puréed into a paste, will take these twists to the next level.

Herbes de Provence Aioli

Ice Cube Tray: Decorative 🎩 Makes about ¾ cup, or about 8–12 shapes

Herbes de Provence is the name for a group of dried seasonings comprising thyme, rosemary, oregano, summer savory, marjoram, parsley, and lavender flowers. Some also include any combination of the following: tarragon, fennel seeds, basil, or mint. You can make your own, but you can also easily buy it in the spice aisle. Aioli is a condiment that stems from the region of Provence as well—it translates to "garlic and oil" in Provençal—so it makes sense to flavor this garlicky homemade mayonnaise with this signature herb mixture.

1 egg

1 tablespoon lemon juice

1 teaspoon garlic powder

¼ cup Herbes de Provence

¼ teaspoon salt

½ cup olive oil

Lay out a decorative ice cube tray of your choice.

In a food processor, place the egg, lemon juice, garlic powder, Herbes de Provence, and salt. Pulse until they are combined.

While the motor is running, add the olive oil in a thin stream. You should see the aioli form almost immediately. Stop the motor once it forms; do not over-process.

Dividing evenly, fill the wells. Cover with parchment paper and freeze, about 3 to 4 hours.

Unmold by turning upside-down on parchment paper and tapping out the segments. Use in a recipe as an accent or present on a cheese or charcuterie tray as a garnish.

THINK OUTSIDE THE TRAY

You can replace the Herbes de Provence with any blend of spices and herbs that you want. Go Italian with oregano, garlic powder, red pepper flakes, basil, and rosemary. Feeling Mexican? Garlic and onion powders, ground cumin, chili powder, paprika, and dried oregano should do the trick. Whatever cuisine you want to suggest, just remember to incorporate dried herbs rather than fresh, as they disperse more easily and evenly in the emulsion.

Ginger-Carrot Vinaigrette

Ice Cube Tray: Mini Grid 🛒 Makes 320 cubes

This dressing is always excellent on a cold, crisp salad. But it's also ideal for dropping into a quick stir-fry, adding to a noodle dish for instant flavor, or marinating light proteins like chicken, fish, or pork.

½ cup chopped fresh carrots

2 tablespoons chopped fresh ginger

1 clove garlic, minced

¼ cup rice vinegar

1 tablespoon soy sauce

2 tablespoons mayonnaise

1 tablespoon sesame oil

½ cup vegetable oil

¼ cup water (optional)

Freshly ground sea salt to taste

Lay out a pair of 160-well, mini grid ice cube trays.

In a food processor, purée the carrots, ginger, and garlic together. Add vinegar, soy sauce, mayonnaise, sesame oil, and vegetable oil. Purée until well combined.

Assess the texture. If you find it too thick, add water until the texture you desire is achieved.

Using a different dropper or turkey baster, or using the Icing Method (see page 7), fill the ice cube tray wells with dressing almost to the top. Don't overfill or ice cubes will be hard to release.

Note: Each mini ice cube tray holds about ¾ of a cup, so you may have a little bit of dressing left over.

Cover with parchment paper and freeze until solid, about 3 to 4 hours. Unmold by cracking the cubes over a piece of parchment paper. Scatter whole over salad or serve defrosted in a bowl.

THINK OUTSIDE THE TRAY

For an extra bite, throw some radish chunks in with the carrots and purée them. You can use any radish, but if you want to stick to the Japanese theme, try some daikon radish. It makes an appealing addition!

Buffalo Blue Cheese Dressing

Ice Cube Tray: Mini Grid 🎩 Makes 320 cubes

Imagine these tiny marbled cubes melting on chicken wings. They not only provide full-on flavor, they also cool those wings right off, so you can eat them right away.

¼ cup Tabasco, divided

½ cup sour cream

½ cup mayonnaise

¼ cup buttermilk

1 tablespoon white vinegar

1 teaspoon lemon juice

5 ounces finely crumbled blue cheese

1 tablespoon minced chervil (or parsley)

Freshly ground sea salt and black pepper to taste

Lay out a pair of 160-well, mini grid ice cube trays.

Using a dropper or turkey baster, very lightly dot and drizzle the bottoms of the ice cube trays with about half of the Tabasco sauce. You want to create a marbled effect when filling the wells.

In a food processor, combine all the ingredients except for the Tabasco sauce. Blend well. Adjust for taste and texture. If too thick and creamy, add more vinegar or lemon juice. If too tangy, add more mayonnaise.

Using the Icing Method, fill the ice cube tray wells with dressing almost to the top. Don't overfill; dairy expands when freezing, plus you need room for the next step.

Drizzle and dot the tops of the wells with the remaining Tabasco sauce. Cover very lightly with parchment paper—this shouldn't smear the sauce if you haven't filled them to the top—and freeze until solid, about 3 to 4 hours.

Note: Each mini ice cube tray holds about ¾ of a cup, so you may have a little bit of dressing left over.

Cover with parchment paper and freeze until solid, about 3 to 4 hours. Unmold by cracking the cubes over a piece of parchment paper. Scatter whole over salad or wings, or serve defrosted in a bowl.

THINK OUTSIDE THE TRAY

There's no reason why you can't freeze other salad dressings this way. These miniature cubes, which are the size of croutons, are also the perfect choice for Caesar salad dressing. They look picture-perfect on top of torn romaine lettuce. And you don't have to worry about whether the dressing has raw egg in it—both yolks and whites freeze well.

Maître d'Hôtel Butter

Ice Cube Tray: Decorative 🎩 Makes about 15 shapes
(depending on size of shape) per stick of butter

Maître d'hôtel butter, a compound including lemon juice and parsley to sharpen and complement the bland creaminess of the dairy, was invented by the French and traditionally prepared tableside. Now it's easy to make ahead of time and freeze. When you use decorative ice cube trays to do so, you can create any shape that you want. And because the butter pats are frozen, they'll hold their shapes for a bit, even as you slide them onto hot, grilled steak, until you get them to the table for presentation.

1 stick unsalted butter, room temperature

1 tablespoon freshly chopped parsley

1 tablespoon freshly chopped dill

1 teaspoon freshly squeezed lemon juice

1 teaspoon dry Colman's mustard

½ teaspoon freshly ground sea salt

½ teaspoon freshly ground black pepper

Lay out a decorative ice cube tray.

In a bowl, combine all ingredients with a spatula or your hands and mix well.

Using a small spoon or your fingers, scoop into the decorative shape ice cube tray wells and smooth the tops with a cake scraper. Freeze until ready to use.

You can also freeze a batch, unmold from the trays to store in airtight containers, and reuse the trays to make more (or something else).

Unmold with your fingers. Present on top of grilled meats, fish or vegetables, or pop on top of a bowl of chipped ice for a great bread-and-butter presentation.

THINK OUTSIDE THE TRAY

Flavor your compound butter with whatever herbs and spices you like. Add a combination of chili pepper, cumin, and cayenne for a smoky, zesty Southwestern edge. Replace the parsley and dill with cilantro and/or culantro and substitute lime juice for the lemon juice for a Caribbean twist. To reference Spain, use paprika, saffron, and blood orange juice. And curries, from Indian to Thai, make incredibly flavored compound butters.

Pistachio-Arugula Pesto

Ice Cube Tray: Honeycomb 🍯 Makes 37 cubes

Pesto is popular with just about everybody, and it's also a pretty foolproof way to preserve a big batch of fresh greens and/or herbs. Because these trays also come with lids, you might be tempted to leave the pesto cubes in the tray for future use rather than unmolding and storing them in a plastic bag. But the garlic may eventually lend the silicone a slight aroma, so it's best to unmold and keep them in plastic after they've formed.

¼ cup unsalted, naturally colored pistachios, shelled

3 cloves garlic

1½ cups packed arugula leaves

Freshly ground sea salt and pepper to taste

½ cup plus ¼ cup olive oil, divided

½ cup Parmesan

THINK OUTSIDE THE TRAY

For different flavors and textures, change the nut base—try traditional pine nuts instead of pistachio, or walnuts, or a combination of several oily tree nuts. You can do the same with the arugula: substitute the more expected basil, try spinach, or mix many greens and herbs together. You can also use flavored olive oils, such as chili, lemon, rosemary, or truffle, to give the pesto an additional lift.

Lay out a 37-well, honeycomb ice cube tray.

In a food processor, pulse the pistachios with the garlic until the mixture resembles wet sand. Add the arugula, salt, and pepper and blend well. While the machine is still running, pour in the ½ cup of olive oil through the tube until the mixture is puréed. Add the Parmesan and purée again.

With a small teaspoon, fill the wells of the ice cube tray, leaving a little bit of room at the tops of the wells. Smooth the wells as best you can, leaving as few air holes as possible.

Fill a dropper or turkey baster with the remaining ¼ cup of olive oil. Add a few drops to the top of each well. This will protect the cubes of pesto from freezer burn.

Cover the tray with plastic wrap and then its own cover. Freeze until solid, about 4 hours.

Note: The olive oil will not freeze clearly but will instead be opaque. This is normal.

Unmold by turning upside-down on parchment paper and tapping out the segments. Use in a recipe or present on a cheese or charcuterie tray.

Green Olive Tapenade

Ice Cube Tray: Honeycomb 🧊 Makes 37 cubes

Tapenade stems from Provence, where the puréed olive dip is popularly served with bread to begin a meal. This version adds gelatin so that it holds its form as a mold, and the little geometric shapes that result give interesting visual appeal to a charcuterie plate or antipasto.

1½ cups green olives, any variety, drained and pitted

1 tablespoon anchovy paste or minced anchovies

1 tablespoon minced capers

1 garlic clove, minced

2 tablespoons fresh lemon juice

2 tablespoons olive oil

2 tablespoons minced Italian parsley

Freshly ground sea salt and black pepper to taste

1 envelope powdered gelatin

Lay out a 37-well honeycomb ice cube tray (or several decorative shapes trays).

In a food processor, add all the ingredients except for the gelatin and purée.

Dissolve one packet of gelatin in a cup of hot water. Add to the olive mixture and stir well.

Spoon the olive mixture into the wells. Cover with parchment paper and refrigerate for 24 hours.

Note: These will melt quickly in the heat, so if you're planning on serving outside, pop them into the freezer for an hour.

Unmold by turning upside-down on parchment paper and tapping out the segments. Use in a recipe or present on a cheese or charcuterie tray.

THINK OUTSIDE THE TRAY

Use different olive varietals for a bouquet of looks. To change up the taste, add a tablespoon of mustard, any type. Dijon or Dusseldorf works well with the strength of the olives and anchovies, and a spicy mustard gives an extra jab to the palate.

House Cocktail Sauce

Ice Cube Tray: Honeycomb 🎩 Makes 37 cubes

When serving chilled seafood, nothing makes it taste better than homemade cocktail sauce. But you don't always have the ingredients on hand—unless, of course, you've kept a batch frozen from the last time you made it. Frozen cocktail sauce cubes also provide an arresting presentation, especially for oysters on the half shell, crab claws, and shrimp.

1½ cups ketchup

3 tablespoons ground horseradish

1 tablespoon freshly squeezed lemon juice

2 teaspoons Worcestershire sauce

1 teaspoon Tabasco sauce (optional)

Freshly ground sea salt and black pepper to taste

Lay out a 37-well, honeycomb ice cube tray.

In a bowl, mix the ketchup, horseradish, lemon juice, Worcestershire sauce, Tabasco sauce, and salt and pepper well.

Use a turkey baster or a spoon to fill the wells of the ice cube tray. Be careful not to overfill.

Place the cover on the tray and set levelly in the freezer. Freeze until solid, about 3 to 4 hours.

Unmold by turning upside-down on parchment paper and tapping out the segments. Use in a recipe or present on a seafood platter as a garnish.

THINK OUTSIDE THE TRAY

For more intensity, use fresh horseradish root or add a pinch of wasabi to the mix. For extra lemony flavor, add some zest as well as the juice. Instead of Tabasco, try sriracha.

Zucchini-Lemon Raita

Ice Cube Tray: Decorative 🧊 Makes about 12 cubes

Raita is usually made with yogurt and cucumbers and is an excellent foil for spicy Indian dishes. Here, I substitute zucchini for the cucumbers, and add a touch of lemon zest. The condiment still cools the overheated palate, but you can use it to pair with anything you like. I think it's ideal with fried foods as well as zesty ones.

½ cup plain yogurt

½ cup grated raw zucchini

½ teaspoon ground coriander

½ teaspoon cumin

½ teaspoon lemon zest

1 tablespoon freshly chopped cilantro

Freshly grated sea salt and black pepper to taste

Lay out a decorative ice cube tray of your choice.

In a bowl, mix all the ingredients together. Allow to sit and blend in the refrigerator for at least 4 hours.

Dividing evenly, fill the wells of the ice cube tray. Do not overfill; this will expand when it freezes. Cover with parchment paper and place in the freezer for 3 to 4 hours.

Unmold with your fingers. Use in a recipe as an accent or present on a cheese or charcuterie tray as a garnish.

THINK OUTSIDE THE TRAY

To give this a Greek flavor (tzatziki) instead of an Indian one, replace the spices and cilantro with dill, add minced garlic, and stir in a tablespoon of lemon juice or white vinegar. If you want to use the traditional cucumbers, keep in mind that they give off a lot of juice when you shred them, so you should drain them before adding them to the yogurt. See the sidebar, How to Thicken Sour Cream Naturally (page 83), for directions.

Sweets

An Array of Chocolates

Ice Cube Tray: Decorative 🎩 Yield dependent on tray used

Yes, you can make chocolate at home. It's actually fairly easy—and even simpler if you have the right tools, such as a funnel, cake scrapers, and a double boiler. Below are several different methods for molding a variety of chocolates.

Quick Molds

1 bag of white, milk, or dark chocolate chips

Lay out any decorative ice cube tray.

Pour the chips in a microwave bowl. Heat for 1 to 2 minutes until thoroughly melted. Stir and pour into a funnel.

Alternatively, heat the water in a double boiler. In the top portion, melt the chips by stirring continuously. When there are no lumps left, pour the chocolate into a funnel.

Position the funnel over the wells and fill them. Cover with parchment or plastic wrap. Refrigerate overnight or 24 hours to set. Before unmolding, use a cake scraper to clean the trays and free them of scraps.

Unmold and serve.

Chocolate from Cocoa

½ cup water

1 cup cocoa powder

6 tablespoons butter, room temperature

½ cup confectioner's sugar

½ teaspoon salt

⅓ cup milk (optional)

In a saucepan, heat the water until just under boiling temperature.

In a food processor, cream the cocoa with the butter until it's an entirely smooth paste. Add the sugar and salt and cream again.

Add the mixture to the water until it's completely dissolved. If you want to keep the chocolate dark, don't add the milk. For milk chocolate, do add the milk. When there are no lumps left, pour the chocolate into the funnel.

Position the funnel over the wells and fill them. Cover with parchment or plastic wrap. Refrigerate overnight or 24 hours to set. Before unmolding, use a cake scraper to clean the trays and free them of scraps.

Unmold with your fingers and serve.

(continued on next page)

White Chocolate

½ cup food-grade cocoa butter, finely chopped

½ cup confectioner's sugar

1½ teaspoons powdered milk

½ teaspoon vanilla extract

Pinch of salt

Lay out any decorative ice cube tray.

Heat the water in a double boiler. In the top portion, melt the cocoa butter until liquefied. Be careful not to burn it.

Add the sugar and powdered milk. Stir until dissolved and no lumps are left. Add the vanilla extract and salt. Stir again. When the white chocolate is smooth, fill the funnel.

Position the funnel over the wells and fill them. Cover with parchment or plastic wrap. Refrigerate overnight or 24 hours to set. Before unmolding, use a cake scraper to clean the trays and free them of scraps.

Unmold with your fingers and serve.

THINK OUTSIDE THE TRAY

Making chocolate from chips is a tremendous birthday party activity for older children who can be trusted not to burn themselves. (It's best if adults handle the funnel and children decorate the end product.) With all the flavors of chips on the market, you don't have to stick to chocolate, either. You can make butterscotch and caramel molds, too. Throw some unsalted almonds, cashews, or macadamia nuts into the ice cube tray wells before you pour in the chocolate. Add sprinkles. You can also mix in fresh fruit to the chocolates before they set. Raspberries, bits of strawberries, blueberries, and slices of bananas are all luscious!

DOUBLE BOILER

Cooking with a double boiler allows you to apply indirect heat to food and is an excellent way to melt solids like chocolate without burning them. You can easily buy double boilers, but if you don't have one and want to use one, you can also rig one by putting two pots of the same size together. Fill the pot that will go underneath with water, and put that on the stove burner. Then place the pot with the food on top of it. The heat is applied to the pot with the water, and the steam from the water heats the pot with the food in it.

COCOA BUTTER

You can't buy cocoa butter in a regular market, and you also can't always buy food-grade cocoa butter in a specialty store. Make sure you know what you're purchasing. Cocoa butter is vegetable fat that's extracted from the cocoa bean, but it has two uses. The first is the edible one, and the second one is for beauty products and skin creams. You wouldn't want to wind up with the latter in your white chocolate! In my opinion, the best way to foolproof your cocoa butter buying is to get it online from a trusted manufacturer, or from a market where you really know the stock.

THINK OUTSIDE THE TRAY

Instead of adding batter to the bottom of the wells, use a piece of graham cracker for the marshmallow to rest on. This will give the cakes a bit of a s'mores flavor. You can also sprinkle crushed graham crackers on top or incorporate chocolate chips to make this extra rich.

Chocolate Marshmallow "Cube-Cakes"

Ice Cube Tray: 2-Inch Square 🧊 Makes 12 "cube-cakes"

Thanks to the marshmallows, these miniature chocolate cakes are sticky and gooey throughout—and I mean that in the best way. The marshmallows aren't a filling but instead melt and disperse themselves throughout the cake. The resulting flavor reminds me of chocolate marshmallow sundaes from my sweets-obsessed youth, spent (as often as possible) at Friendly's, back then the only ice cream parlor in my small town. Now I bake these to eat *with* ice cream, which takes them to a whole new level.

1¼ cups flour

¾ cup sugar

½ cup unsweetened cocoa powder

½ teaspoon salt

1 teaspoon baking powder

1 teaspoon baking soda

1 egg

¼ cup oil

½ cup water, room temperature

½ cup milk

1 teaspoon white vinegar

6 regular-sized marshmallows, halved

Lay out a pair of 6-well, 2-inch square ice cube trays. Spray or brush them with cooking oil or line them with cupcake wrappers.

Preheat the oven to 350°F.

In a bowl, mix the flour, sugar, cocoa, salt, baking powder, and baking soda together.

In another bowl, whisk the egg with the oil, water, milk, and vinegar. Add the mixture to the dry ingredients and whisk for 2 minutes or until the batter is smooth with no lumps.

Add a teaspoon or two of batter to the bottom of each well. Drop in half of one marshmallow into each well. Cover with batter until the wells are ¾ of the way filled. Do not overfill; the cakes will rise when baked.

Place in the oven and bake for 20 to 25 minutes or until a toothpick inserted into the cake comes out clean. Allow to cool completely before unmolding with a mini spatula. Serve plain, frost them, or top with ice cream.

Amaretto-Raisin Bread Pudding Bites

Ice Cube Tray: 1-Inch Square 🧊 Makes 15 miniature bread puddings

Bread pudding is always a phenomenal treat that's surprisingly simple to make. Whether you're making this for your family, your guests, or for yourself, you'll be enamored of these adorable cubes.

½ cup raisins

¼ cup Amaretto

15 cubes of stale French bread, cut slightly smaller than a square inch

1 cup milk

1 egg

½ cup light brown sugar

½ teaspoon vanilla extract

½ teaspoon cinnamon

•••••••••••••••••••••••••

THINK OUTSIDE THE TRAY

Instead of raisins and Amaretto, try dried cherries and bourbon, or dried cranberries and rum, or dried apricots and limoncello. The combination of fruit and alcohol is up to you.

Lay out a 15-well, 1-inch square ice cube tray. Spray or brush them with cooking oil or melted butter. Preheat the oven to 350°F.

In a small bowl, combine the raisins with the Amaretto. Set aside to marinate.

In another bowl, add the cubes of bread. Pour the milk over them. Allow the bread to absorb the milk. Set aside.

In a third bowl, beat the egg with the sugar, vanilla extract, and cinnamon. Whisk. Add the raisins and Amaretto and whisk again.

Pour the egg mixture over the bread and stir gently to combine. Allow the bread to soak in the mixture for 10 to 15 minutes.

Place one cube of bread in each well of the tray. Pour the remaining egg-milk mixture over the cubes of bread until the wells of the trays are filled. Place in the oven and bake for 30 to 35 minutes or until the tops have browned and the liquid has set.

Slide a dull knife blade around the edges of the squares to loosen them. Unmold carefully with a mini spatula. Serve plain or top with ice cream.

Apricot Crumb Coffee Cake

Ice Cube Tray: 2-Inch Square 🎩 Makes 12 coffee cakes

This updated standard, which used to be in practically every bakery and coffee shop around, is perfect for baking in ice cube trays. It cooks at a low oven temperature, and the trays do the portioning and edging for you.

For the topping:
8 tablespoons (1 stick) butter, melted

¼ cup sugar

¼ cup dark brown sugar

1 teaspoon cinnamon

¼ teaspoon salt

4 tablespoons apricot jam

1½ –1¾ cups flour

For the cake:
1¾ cup flour

½ cup sugar

½ teaspoon baking soda

¼ teaspoon salt

6 tablespoons cold butter, cut into chunks

1 egg

1 egg yolk

½ cup sour cream

1 teaspoon vanilla extract

1 teaspoon almond extract

For the garnish:
¼ cup confectioners' sugar

Lay out a pair of 6-well, 2-inch square ice cube trays. Spray or brush them with cooking oil. Preheat the oven to 325°F.

In a bowl, combine the melted butter, sugar, brown sugar, cinnamon, and salt. Whisk in the apricot jam. Add the flour until it forms a sticky ball. Set aside.

In a food processor or standing mixer, combine the flour, sugar, baking soda, and salt. While the motor is running on low speed, add the chunks of butter until the mixture pills. The dough should look crumbly.

Add the egg, egg yolk, sour cream, vanilla extract, and almond extract and combine. The batter should fluff up.

Dividing evenly, fill the wells halfway up.

Take the topping and divide it in half. Use one half per tray. Break it apart into chunks the size of jelly beans and fill the remaining space of the wells.

Place the trays in the oven and bake for 30 to 35 minutes or until a toothpick inserted into the cake comes out clean. After the cakes cool completely, dust with confectioners' sugar. To unmold, insert a dull knife or mini spatula and loosen the cakes from the sides of the wells. Serve plain or pair with ice cream.

THINK OUTSIDE THE TRAY

Any flavor jam will provide a nice elevation to this coffee cake. Or forego the fruit and mix in chocolate chips to the topping dough.

Chewy Granola Drops

Ice Cube Tray: Mini Sphere 🎩 Makes 36 granola drops

You've no doubt seen granola bites in the store. My daughter suggested that we try making our own, and it was a fun, hands-on activity that we already repeated just because we liked the result so much. These little round balls are just plain irresistible!

¼ cup oats

2 tablespoons chopped unsalted walnuts

2 tablespoons chopped unsalted almonds

1 tablespoon maple syrup

1 tablespoon canola oil

¼ teaspoon cinnamon

¼ teaspoon salt

2 tablespoons dried cranberries

1 tablespoon honey

2 tablespoons mini chocolate chips

Lay out a 36-well, mini sphere ice cube tray. Spray or brush them with cooking oil.

Preheat the oven to 300°F.

Line a baking tray with parchment paper.

In a bowl, mix the oats, almonds, and walnuts together. In another bowl, mix the maple syrup, canola oil, cinnamon, and salt together.

Add the oat mixture to the maple syrup mixture and stir to coat. Spread out the oats in a single layer on the baking sheet and place it into the oven.

Bake for 10 minutes. Remove and stir. Bake for another 10 minutes or until granola is turning golden brown.

Remove from the oven. When granola is cool enough to handle but not set, transfer into a bowl. Add the cranberries and honey. Mix until combined. Lightly fold in the chocolate chips.

Dividing evenly, fill the wells of the tray. Allow granola to set for 4 hours before unmolding with your fingers.

THINK OUTSIDE THE TRAY

The best thing about granola is that it's customizable. Add sunflower seeds, subtract almonds. Don't like cinnamon? Love coconut? It's all up to you. Just follow the general guidelines: Don't include dried fruit until after the granola is baked—it will burn—and if you want chocolate chips to retain their integrity, wait until it's cool before integrating.

Honey-Walnut Phyllo Cups

Ice Cube Tray: 2-Inch Sphere 🔲 Makes 12 pastries

That roll of phyllo dough left over from making the Mixed Mushroom Beggar's Purse (page 105) recipe comes in handy here to make a quick, tasty dessert. And when I say quick, I mean you can actually prepare this in 10 minutes.

1 roll phyllo dough, thawed

⅓ cup unsalted walnuts

3 tablespoons honey

½ teaspoon cinnamon

Lay out a pair of 6-well, 2-inch sphere ice cube trays (or substitute decorative trays that have deep wells). Spray or brush them with cooking oil.

Preheat the oven to 350°F.

Spray or brush a single phyllo sheet with oil on both sides, then lay it on parchment paper. Repeat with another sheet and lay it directly on top. Repeat until you have a stack of 10 sheets.

In a bowl, crush the walnuts into very small nuggets. Add the honey and cinnamon and mix.

Cut the phyllo dough into 4 even rows. Cut the 4 rows into thirds. You should have 12 squares. (If you're using a decorative tray, judge for yourself how to cut the dough so that it fits.) Push the center of one dough square gently into the center of one well. The edges of the dough should poke up over the well. Repeat until all wells are filled.

Fill the wells with the honeyed walnuts.

Place in the oven and bake until the pastry is golden brown, about 15 to 20 minutes. Allow to cool completely before unmolding with tongs. To serve, garnish with dusted cinnamon.

THINK OUTSIDE THE TRAY

You can replace the walnuts with any nuts. Pistachios do really well here, as do almonds. Brazil nuts are also delicious. Try a mixture of all four. Macadamia nuts make this extra rich. Peanuts, however, tend to dominate.

Sorbet–Ice Cream "Creamsicles"

Ice Cube Tray: Layered ⬭ Makes 8 "Creamsicles"

I won't lie—the layered ice cube tray is entertaining and presents beautiful cubes, but it does require commitment. The wells have four graduated sections, so to work with it in terms of freezing or molding, you have to devote four parts of your day to it. It's easiest, for this recipe, if you microwave a little bit of the sorbet and ice cream at a time, just to soften it, to fill the layers.

½ cup colored sprinkles, divided

1 pint vanilla ice cream, softened to the point of melting

1 pint sorbet, any flavor, softened to the point of melting

8 miniature popsicle sticks

Lay out an 8-well, layered ice cube tray.

Dividing evenly, fill the bottoms of the wells with ¼ cup of the colored sprinkles.

Starting with the very soft vanilla ice cream, fill the lowest graduated layer of the wells. Smooth the layers with the smallest cake scraper. Place in the freezer for 1 hour.

Remove from the freezer. Fill the next graduated layer with very soft sorbet. Return the tray to the freezer for 1 hour.

Remove from the freezer. Dividing evenly, distribute the remaining ¼ cup of the colored sprinkles. Then fill the next graduated layer with very soft vanilla ice cream. Return the tray to the freezer for 1 hour.

Remove from the freezer. Fill the next graduated layer with very soft sorbet. Insert miniature popsicle sticks. Return the tray to the freezer for 1 hour.

If the "Creamsicles" don't unmold easily, run a hot but dull knife around the edges to help ease them out.

THINK OUTSIDE THE TRAY

You don't have to stick to the sorbet-ice cream combination. You can put together these graduated pops using any flavors of ice cream, and with chocolate sprinkles, chopped nuts, or any kind of crushed candy between the layers.

Frozen Jell-O Parfait

Ice Cube Tray: Layered 🎩 Makes 16 parfaits

This very sweet dessert reminds me of my childhood, when we used to have canned fruit cocktail every so often as a treat. No one wanted the pears, and of course we fought over the cherries. Out of respect for those memories, I didn't include pears here. But you're more than welcome to add them if you like.

1 packet cherry Jell-O

1 can sliced peaches, chopped with juice

1 cup whipped cream

1 can crushed pineapple, with juice

Lay out a pair of 8-well, layered ice cube trays.

Prepare the Jell-O according to directions. Fill the lowest graduated layer with the Jell-O and place in the refrigerator to set, up to 4 hours. (You will have extra Jell-O, so see I Heart Jell-O shots, page 11, for what to do with the rest.)

Remove from the refrigerator and fill the next graduated layer with chopped peaches and juice. Place in the freezer for 1 hour.

Remove from the freezer and fill the next graduated layer with whipped cream. Place in the freezer for 1 hour.

Remove from the freezer and fill the top layer with pineapple and juice. Place in the freezer for 1 hour.

Unmold and serve on a plate. If the parfaits don't unmold easily, run a hot knife around the edges to help ease them out.

THINK OUTSIDE THE TRAY

Any flavor Jell-O is fine on the bottom, and any kind of fruit or juice will work in the frozen sections. The key here is not to add more Jell-O on top of the molded Jell-O, because hot liquid can melt what's already set underneath. If you're really crafty and have a cake slicer, you can slip in a layer of pound cake, sponge cake, or angel food cake, which makes this truly sumptuous.

Cereal Treats

Ice Cube Tray: 2-Inch Square and Traditional 🎩

Makes 12 large squares and 36 smaller squares

Rice Krispy Treats are so yesterday. Take your gooey marshmallow goodness to a whole new level—and array of shapes and sizes—by making them in the ice cube tray of your choice. This is a fun, rainy day activity that yields instant results for bored kids and adults who never lost that insatiable sweet tooth.

3 tablespoons butter

10 ounces marshmallows

6 cups cereal of choice

Lay out a pair of 6-well, 2-inch square ice cube tray and a pair of 18-well, square trays.

Spray the trays lightly with cooking oil.

In a saucepan, melt the butter. Stir in the marshmallow until they are melted as well. Remove from the heat.

Add the cereal and mix well. Using your hands and with the help of wax paper, fill the wells evenly. This can be sticky and tricky, but the results are worth it.

Once the wells are filled, allow the cool and set. Unmold bit by bit or serve all at once.

THINK OUTSIDE THE TRAY

Any cereal will work here, depending on how colorful and sweet you like it. Smaller flakes and puffed rice combinations work best, but loops also can be tamed into various molds. Don't care for sugary cereals? Try making this with granola, nuts, dark chocolate, and coconut. The marshmallow binder will still add that candy-like coating, but the texture will be coarser and denser.

Oreo Crust Mini Cheesecakes

Ice Cube Tray: 1-Inch Square 🧊 Makes 15 miniature cheesecakes

Cheesecake is such a versatile dessert! It's also one of the easier recipes to make in ice cube trays. This is why I decided to make it two ways. You can choose to use the baked version, which I like to top after it cools with jam or fruit, or the no-bake version, which is best when the fruit is mixed in the way you do with yogurt. Then simply freeze and enjoy. Think of them as winter and summer versions, if you like.

Baked Version

1 cup Oreo crumbs (10 cookies)

4 tablespoons melted butter

4 ounces cream cheese

4 ounces mascarpone

1 egg

⅓ cup sugar

½ teaspoon vanilla extract

½ cup strawberry jam

Lay out a 15-well, 1-inch square ice cube tray.

Preheat the oven to 350°F.

In a bowl, mix Oreo crumbs and butter together. Divide evenly—about a generous ½ teaspoon for each—and press into the bottoms of the ice cube tray wells.

In a food processor, blend the cream cheese and mascarpone with the egg, sugar, and vanilla extract. Again dividing evenly—about 2 teaspoons—drop the mixture into the ice cube tray wells. Smooth the tops.

Bake for 20 to 25 minutes or until the tops of the cheesecakes are lightly browned and starting to crack. Remove from the oven and cool.

The cheesecakes shrink as they cook. This leaves plenty of room for topping. Top with strawberry jam before or after unmolding depending on how you want to serve them.

No-Bake Freezer Version

Ice Cube Tray: 1-Inch Square 🎩 Makes 15 miniature frozen cheesecakes

1 cup Oreo crumbs (10 cookies)

4 tablespoons melted butter

15 ounces ricotta cheese

⅓ cup sugar

1 teaspoon vanilla extract

1 teaspoon lemon juice

½ –1 cup blueberries

Lay out a 15-well, 1-inch square ice cube tray.

In a bowl, mix Oreo crumbs and butter together. Divide evenly—about a generous ½ teaspoon for each—and press into the bottoms of the ice cube tray wells.

Freeze the tray with the crust in it while you prepare the filling.

In a bowl or food processor, whip the ricotta cheese, sugar, vanilla extract, and lemon juice. Gently fold in blueberries, keeping them whole.

Again dividing evenly—about 2 teaspoons for each—drop the mixture into the ice cube tray wells. Smooth the tops.

Note: You may have a little filling left over. It's fine to eat raw, as there are no eggs in it.

Freeze until solid, about 4 hours.

To unmold, insert a dull knife or mini spatula and loosen the cakes from the sides of the wells. Serve plain or top with whipped cream.

•⸳•⸳•ᴥ•⸳ᵛ⸳ᵗ ⸳ᵛ•ᴥ•ᵛ⸳ᵗ⸳•⸳•⸳ ⸳•ᵃ ᶠ•ᴥ•⸳ ᵛ⸳•ᵗ•⸳⸳•ᵗ ⸳⸳ ᵗᵛ⸳•ᵗ•ᵖ

THINK OUTSIDE THE TRAY

For different flavors, trade out the Oreos and jams. Try Golden Oreos with raspberry jam, or chocolate mint Oreos with orange marmalade. You can also substitute brown sugar for white sugar; the brown sugar adds a richer flavor.

Miami-Style Key Lime Pie

Ice Cube Tray: 1-Inch Square 🎩 Makes 30 key lime pies

This classic key lime pie recipe is easily divided in half or doubled, depending on how many of these luscious little squares you want to make. They are irresistible at a party or on a buffet table—watch how quickly they disappear!

1 cup graham cracker crumbs

¼ cup sugar

4 tablespoons melted butter

4 egg yolks

1 teaspoon key lime zest

1 can (14-ounces) sweetened condensed milk

1 cup fresh key lime juice

•··•\·\·'·|·•'\·''·/·'·\·A·•

THINK OUTSIDE THE TRAY

Experiment with different citruses, such as Meyer lemon or mandarin orange. Make a variety and serve them all at once so that guests can experience a spectrum of flavors. You can also serve them plain or top them with anything from confectioners' sugar to little puffs of whipped cream.

Lay out a pair of 15-well, 1-inch square ice cube trays.

Preheat the oven to 350°F.

In a bowl, mix graham cracker crumbs, sugar, and butter together. Divide evenly—about a generous ½ teaspoon for each—and press into the bottoms of the ice cube tray wells.

Place in the oven and bake until the crust sets, about 8 to 10 minutes.

In a food processor or high-speed mixer, blend the egg yolks and key lime zest until frothy, about 5 minutes. While the motor is running, slowly add the condensed milk. Repeat with the lime juice on a lower speed or while pulsing until the mixture is just combined. Do not over-blend.

Again dividing evenly, drop the mixture—about 2 teaspoons each—into the ice cube tray wells.

Return to the oven and bake for another 20 minutes. Check to see if the tops are set; if not, bake for 5-minute increments until they are done. Remove from the oven and cool. Refrigerate or freeze for 4 hours until unmolding.

To unmold, insert a dull knife or mini spatula and loosen the pies from the sides of the wells. Serve plain or top with whipped cream.

White Chocolate-Rum Blondies

Ice Cube Tray: 1-Inch Square 🎩 Makes 15–30 blondies

This blondie recipe results in some seriously rich sweets. They're ideal as these little bites for that reason, but you can also make them in bigger trays, like the 2-inch square, if you want to have more heft.

1 stick unsalted butter, melted

2 tablespoons dark rum

1 tablespoon molasses

1 egg, beaten

1 teaspoon vanilla extract

1 cup light brown sugar

1 pinch salt

1 cup flour

¼ cup white chocolate chips

Lay out one or a pair of 15-well, 1-inch square ice cube trays, depending on how thin or thick you want your blondies. If you want thicker blondies, use one tray. If you want thin ones, use two. Spray or brush them with cooking oil.

Preheat the oven to 350°F.

In a bowl, combine the butter, rum, molasses, egg, and vanilla extract.

Stir in the sugar and salt until they dissolve. Stir in the flour until it dissolves. Mix well. The batter should be thick and sticky. Stir in the chocolate chips.

Dividing evenly, fill the wells. Place in the oven and bake for 20 to 25 minutes or until a toothpick comes out clean.

To unmold, insert a dull knife or mini spatula and loosen the blondies from the sides of the wells. Serve plain or top with ice cream.

•·.·•·*·•·'·*·•·'·*·•·'·*·•·'·*·•·'·*·•·'·*·•·'·*·•·'·*·•·

THINK OUTSIDE THE TRAY

This recipe takes to additions and substitutions with no trouble at all. I personally love to add dried cherries to these, but you might prefer cranberries, raisins, chopped apricots, or dates. Change the white chocolate to milk or dark. Include coconut if you want a tropical flavor—that goes superbly with the rum. And speaking of rum, you don't have to include alcohol, or you can change the kind. Try a coffee, citrus, or nut liqueur for vibrancy.

Mango Flan

Ice Cube Tray: 1-Inch Square 🎩 Makes 15 mango flan

Flan is one of those desserts that looks truly impressive and seems difficult to make. But in reality, it's fairly simple. Because I'm lucky enough to have mango trees here in Miami, I can make my own mango nectar. But you can find it easily enough in the juice aisle (or sometimes in the imported goods aisle) of your local supermarket. If you live in a big city, you can also get fresh mango juice in the refrigerated part of the market, or even a mango to juice from the produce section.

1 cup sugar

½ cup mango nectar

4 eggs

1 can (14 ounces) sweetened condensed milk

1 can (12 ounces) evaporated milk

1 teaspoon vanilla extract

1 teaspoon almond extract

Preheat the oven to 350°F.

Lay out a pair of 15-well, 1-inch square ice cube trays.

In a saucepan, melt the sugar into the mango nectar over a low flame until syrupy. Remove from heat. Dividing evenly, pour the mixture into the wells, coating the sides and bottoms.

In a bowl or food processor, beat the eggs. Add the condensed and evaporated milks and vanilla and almond extracts and beat until smooth.

Again dividing evenly, drop the mixture—about 2 teaspoons each—into the ice cube tray wells. Smooth the tops.

Cover with foil, place in the oven, and bake for 30 minutes. Remove from the oven and cool. To unmold, insert a dull knife or mini spatula and loosen the flan from the sides of the wells. Invert on a serving plate when ready to unmold so that you don't lose any of the nectar.

THINK OUTSIDE THE TRAY

If you remove the mango from the equation and melt the sugar by itself, you have traditional caramel flan. But you can add any tropical juice to achieve that extra little tang—pineapple, passion fruit, or guava are all perfect for this recipe.

Cinnamon-Apple Pancakes

Ice Cube Tray: 2-Inch Sphere 🎩 Makes 24 pancakes

These baked pancakes take the best of the fall harvest apples, pare them down into hand-sized portions via the spherical ice cube tray, and provide your family and friends with a just-right slice of autumnal spice. No need to worry about leftovers—in fact, you may have to make more than one batch!

¼ cup flour

2 teaspoons sugar, divided

¼ teaspoon salt

¼ teaspoon baking powder

2 eggs

½ cup milk

1 tablespoon butter, melted

½ teaspoon vanilla extract

1 apple, peeled and thinly sliced and chopped into thumbnail-sized pieces

1 teaspoon lemon juice

½ teaspoon cinnamon

¼ teaspoon nutmeg

THINK OUTSIDE THE TRAY

The basic pancake recipe can be enhanced with any kind of sturdy fruit. Pears also work, as do stone fruit like peaches, although they're a little juicier and softer, so you have to account for that. You can also add chocolate chips and bananas—a house favorite!—or top with *dulce de leche*.

Lay out a pair of 6-well, 2-inch sphere ice cube tray. Spray or brush them with cooking oil.

Preheat the oven to 375°F.

In a bowl, combine the flour, 1 teaspoon sugar, salt, and baking powder. Stir to combine.

In another bowl, combine eggs, milk, melted butter, and vanilla extract. Add to the dry ingredients and mix to form a batter. Set aside for 30 minutes.

Meanwhile, in a bowl, combine the apples with the lemon juice, cinnamon, nutmeg, and 1 teaspoon sugar. Stir until well combined.

Line the wells of the ice cube trays with about 1 teaspoon of apples each. Place in the oven and bake for 5 minutes or until apples start to soften and become aromatic. Remove from the oven.

Pour 1 tablespoon of the batter in each well and return to the oven to bake for 20 to 25 minutes or until each pancake is cooked through and crisp at the edges. These will puff up like soufflés in the oven and then fall as you take them out and they lose their air. To unmold, wait until that happens, then loosen them gently with a mini spatula from the bottoms of the trays. They should come away easily.

Repeat the process until all apples and batter are used. Serve several at a time with confectioner's sugar or ice cream. Refrigerate leftovers; the egg content makes them susceptible to spoilage.

About the Author

A Miami-based writer and poet, **Jen Karetnick** is the author/coauthor of 18 books and anthologies. She works as the dining critic for *Miami Magazine*, and her freelance articles appear widely. Visit her at https://jkaretnick.com.

Acknowledgments

I would like to thank my husband, Jon, and children, Zoe and Remy, for lending their imaginations and appetites to this project, and for not kicking me out of the house for melting various objects in the oven.

A huge thank-you to Stacy Shugerman for figuring out the best lighting in the house, among other photography tasks, and to Maria del Carmen Martinez for eating random, oddly shaped experiments.

I extend an enormous amount of gratitude to Jessica Alvarez and the team at BookEnds Literary Agency for their invaluable assistance.

This book wouldn't have been possible without Nicole Frail, editor extraordinaire, who brought this idea to the table (and freezer and oven). Thank you to her and everyone at Skyhorse Publishing who worked so hard creating, editing, designing, and proofreading these pages. I appreciate you!

As always, nothing would ever be accomplished without the support of immediate and extended family. I am truly indebted to my parents Naomi and Barry, my in-laws Toby and Joel, all my brothers- and sisters-in-law and their kids who cheer me on no matter what. I especially appreciate my sister and partner in crime, Betsy, who is always game for an adventure.

Conversion Charts

METRIC AND IMPERIAL CONVERSIONS

(These conversions are rounded for convenience)

Ingredient	Cups/Tablespoons/Teaspoons	Ounces	Grams/Milliliters
Butter	1 cup/ 16 tablespoons/ 2 sticks	8 ounces	230 grams
Cheese, shredded	1 cup	4 ounces	110 grams
Cornstarch	1 tablespoon	0.3 ounce	8 grams
Cream cheese	1 tablespoon	0.5 ounce	14.5 grams
Flour, all-purpose	1 cup/1 tablespoon	4.5 ounces/0.3 ounce	125 grams/8 grams
Flour, whole wheat	1 cup	4 ounces	120 grams
Fruit, dried	1 cup	4 ounces	120 grams
Fruits or veggies, chopped	1 cup	5 to 7 ounces	145 to 200 grams
Fruits or veggies, puréed	1 cup	8.5 ounces	245 grams
Honey, maple syrup, or corn syrup	1 tablespoon	0.75 ounce	20 grams
Liquids: cream, milk, water, or juice	1 cup	8 fluid ounces	240 milliliters
Oats	1 cup	5.5 ounces	150 grams
Salt	1 teaspoon	0.2 ounces	6 grams
Spices: cinnamon, cloves, ginger, or nutmeg (ground)	1 teaspoon	0.2 ounce	5 milliliters
Sugar, brown, firmly packed	1 cup	7 ounces	200 grams
Sugar, white	1 cup/1 tablespoon	7 ounces/0.5 ounce	200 grams/12.5 grams
Vanilla extract	1 teaspoon	0.2 ounce	4 grams

OVEN TEMPERATURES

Fahrenheit	Celsius	Gas Mark
225°	110°	¼
250°	120°	½
275°	140°	1
300°	150°	2
325°	160°	3
350°	180°	4
375°	190°	5
400°	200°	6
425°	220°	7
450°	230°	8

Index